IDOL LIMERENCE

The Art of Loving BTS as Phenomena

Wallea Eaglehawk

REVOLUTIONARIES

Brisbane, Australia

Copyright © 2020 Wallea Eaglehawk

Any properly footnoted quotation of up to 500 sequential words may be used without permission, as long as the total number of words quoted does not exceed 2000. Institutions may reproduce up to one chapter total for educational purposes. All other permissions can be requested in writing from Revolutionaries.

ISBN 978-0-6487999-9-3

Cover artwork by Amanda Capshaw [@_ajmakesart]
Book design and typesetting by Paula Pomer

The monologue Like Butter was written at Writing Place in 2019 and co-published by Carclew, Country Arts SA and Currency Press in This Was Urgent Yesterday in 2020.

First published in 2020

Revolutionaries
Brisbane, Australia
www.revolutionaries.com.au

DREAM

Prologue: 8

Echo walked the tree-lined paths that snaked through the sprawling gardens of an estate just outside of the city. She had arrived at the main house just moments before, heart in her throat, only to be directed to follow the cobblestones until they met the river.

Echo had thought about this moment many times over the past three months, and many more times on the plane trip which made hours feel like years. She had planned her outfit over and over, she changed her hair until she couldn't change it any more. Though she had been dreaming of this moment, preparing for a lifetime, she was now certain nothing could ready her. Just like the heart that beat through her chest, she was racing towards an unknown future faster than ever before.

Echo could see someone up ahead, between the trees just beyond the bend in the path. Time stood still and in the blink of an eye, she deduced who it must be. Time stood still but her feet moved her forward, nothing was stopping her now.

Her phone buzzed lightly in her hand: a message.
Are you here? it read.
"I'm here."

She stood behind him now.
Trembling.
Waiting.
He turned around and smiled, so wide his cheeks nearly eclipsed his eyes which turned upwards in greeting.
"오랜만이에요," he said softly.
Echo's breath caught in her chest.
He waited.
Watching.
Soft hair falling in his eyes as they sparkled in the early morning light.
Echo grinned, exhaling.
"Hi Namjoon," she looked down ever so slightly, the intensity of his stare too much to handle, "it has been a while."
"Are you ready?" He tilted his head towards the clearing.
A soft murmur of voices she hadn't noticed before carried over on the wind.
Echo nodded, feeling her heart jump up and down.
They walked side by side, off the cobbled path, to an expanse of grass next to the rapidly moving river. Echo tried not to stare at him while they walked, painfully aware of his existence just out of the corner of her eye.
She turned her head slightly, allowing her eyes to find him.
Namjoon's pace slowed as his head turned in a covert operation of his own.
Their eyes met.
They looked away, smiling.
The light shone differently here.
As they neared the clearing the rising sun was so bright that everything looked a fresh white.
Echo's step faltered when she saw them.
Six figures stood clumped together, quiet falling over the group as all eyes moved to her.
Namjoon joined them as they formed a circle.
A gap for Echo.

Prologue: 8

He counted the heads.
1.
2.
3.
4.
5.
6.
And himself.
7.
He looked over to Echo, still hesitating at the edge of the group.

They all turned to look at her, nervous energy radiating.

They smiled, nodded their heads in greeting. Echo needed no introduction, they had been waiting for this moment as long as she had.

She took a step forward, completing the circle.

8, Namjoon nodded his head.

"Everyone's here," he smiled, relieved.

So, Echo thought to herself as she looked around at the familiar faces, *this is BTS*.

"Are you ready?" he asked, eyes meeting each of the members.

The tension was palpable.

Namjoon shifted his focus to Echo, they were standing opposite one another.

Neither knew what was to come, but they were ready.

"It's time."

The group took one last look at one another.

Calm.

Serene.

"So, Echo," chortled Hoseok, "what exactly do we do now?"

The group laughed.

Echo smiled.

"We leap, of course."

Love

As if we were waiting, we bloom until we ache
—Serendipity, BTS

'Love is a many splendored thing' says wide-eyed Christian standing on top of the elephant house just outside of the Moulin Rouge in Paris, 1899. Earlier that night he had fallen in love with Satine, the star of the Moulin Rouge, and after she briefly mistook him for a wealthy Duke, he was rushing to convince her of why they should be lovers. A classic romance narrative, a man has spied a woman of angelic beauty and grace from across a room and has fallen in love in the space of a beat. A true renaissance man, Christian resorts to serenading Satine with a medley of songs from 70 years in the future. The strong-willed, fiery Satine goes from 'there's no way, 'cos you can't pay' to 'how wonderful life is now you're in the world' in just a few minutes. Amidst fireworks and crescendos, the ill-fated couple, like countless cis-gendered protagonists before them, profess their undying love. Their actions reinforce the status quo of what love looks like in popular culture.

This form of love is inherently romantic; tropes like these have been splayed across screens and pages globally since the creation of the first romance novel. This boy-meets-girl scenario is bottled and sold; a hot commodity. One that provides escapism and lets one dream of being swept off their feet by someone good looking, of financial means, or if you're Gossip Girl's Chuck Bass, both. But is it an accurate representation of real life? According to sociologist Anthony Giddens, romantic love introduces the idea of a narrative as a form of identity into an individual's life. In the late eighteenth century this emerging concept coincided with the release of the first romance novel, the first form of mass media. If this is true then we can start to see that, in many ways, life imitates art, especially when it comes to the romantic narrative.

Echo, a young millennial, would sit and stare at the screen while the videotape played on repeat. *Moulin Rouge* had been on high rotation since its release a year earlier in 2001. At the age of 9, Echo had seen all of Baz Luhrmann's movies in the *red curtain* series: Strictly Ballroom where the accents were undoubtedly Australian and cringe-worthy; Romeo and Juliet which taught more of Shakespeare than Echo would learn in her 11 years of schooling, and finally; Moulin Rouge, the most spectacular display of unrequited love with an all-singing, all-dancing cast that transported Echo to a place she'd much rather be. Echo's heart would soar with each rising note. Although there was a lot that went over Echo's head, what she knew for certain was what love looked like. Love was a racing heart and a red dress, but above all else, love grew through adversity and conquered all. Perhaps what Echo loved most about love, but so often ignored, was that this kind of love was doomed to die. A transient love, brighter than any star that burnt out long before its time, now that was the love that Echo wanted. Love for Echo was like a flower growing through a crack in a wall; beautiful and determined, against all the odds it not only survives, but flourishes.

If The Beatles are correct and love is indeed all we need, what exactly is it? Love can perhaps be best understood as an emotion, something that we all feel. Apart from that, though, it can be hard to pinpoint just what love is. Experts are divided, some saying love is what we use to determine who to procreate with, others say that love is a social construct. According to ancient Greek thinkers, there are over seven types of love ranging from Eros, a lustful love, to Agape, an unconditional love for humanity. Not only is love an emotion, but it's also a set of chemicals released in the body and brain: testosterone and estrogen; dopamine, norepinephrine and serotonin; oxytocin and vasopressin. Each set of chemicals drive lust, attraction and attachment. These chemical reactions influence one's actions and manifest as a broad spectrum of positive emotions: happiness, overwhelm, elation, excitement and euphoria.

The concept of love has evolved over time, shaped by different cultural understandings and collective experiences throughout the world. Not only does the human race shape how love looks and operates through individual actions that follow similar patterns, but they shape love through other socially constructed means, the most powerful of which is mass-media. Through what we consume we are taught that there is one kind of love that everyone needs to feel worthy; the romantic love of another. It is argued that romantic love is unrealistic, unattainable, a flash in the pan. It is argued that there is a different kind of love that is true and pure, the long-lasting kind that builds and grows over time. Michael Novak put it best when suggesting that perhaps romance is a longing for love itself; the desire to be in love and be loved in return, to be showered with love and shout it from the rooftops. Perhaps that is the essence of love, a love for love itself. And, according to Sia, to be human is to love. So it is only human to want romance, and it's only capitalism which packages romance in mass-produced media content for the whole family to enjoy.

At this point in her life, Echo only knew two kinds of love; Storge, a love for family, and Ludus, a playful child-like love

Love

accompanied by dancing and laughter. Echo loved her parents, but most of all Echo loved her friend whose name she carved into the dining table, hoping the rules of Beetlejuice applied, except in a romantic way where they'd love Echo back if their name was inscribed three times. Echo called her friend many names, they spoke in code over the telephone, leaving secret messages on their parents' answering machines after school. Echo called him Lemons, Apples, Oranges. One day Echo changed his name without telling him, so when she said 'Lemons' in hushed tones down the landline it meant 'I love you'. Echo loved that about words, they could carry her feelings five blocks over in a heartbeat, hiding behind the name of a fruit. Every time Echo said his code name her love grew, except his name was now Narcissus, and just like the movies Echo loved so dearly, there was no happy ending in sight.

Happiness for Echo was walking around the swampland near her home with Narcissus, talking about the trees, the water, the ducks and the cracks in the path. Excitement for Echo was hearing that Narcissus broke up with his girlfriend, knowing that they would have more time to talk on the phone all through the night. Elation was the well-laid plans, many months in the making for Echo's 12th birthday camping adventure, coming to fruition. It would be Echo, Narcissus and two of their friends so deeply friend-zoned that Echo felt they weren't going to destabilise the celebration and swoop Narcissus away as others always had. Overwhelm, for Echo was her thoughts running into one another and the unbeating heart when Narcissus professes his love for her friend while they all lie on camp beds in the freezing winter cabin. It was never Echo. The Beetlejuice trick didn't work; it didn't matter how many times Narcissus's name was carved, he'd never love Echo back. Euphoria, when Narcissus moved his head next to Echo's and whispered 'don't worry, I'll always love you', still holding someone else's hand.

How we love is directly linked to how we relate to others.

Idol Limerence

How and who we love shapes our identity just as our identity influences how love is constructed and experienced in our lives. Our identity is the link between our personal experiences, how we feel and what we think, and the social world, which is comprised of varying social, cultural, economic and environmental influences. Identity, just like love and romance, is shaped not only by the world, external factors, but also, our identity. The way we experience love and romance exists on a unique, personal level. Sociologist Erving Goffman believes it is through everyday interactions and conversations that we shape our identities. Goffman's use of theatrical metaphor means that all the world's a stage and each of us are actors, telling stories that are comprised of defining moments and characteristics we have hand-selected to best represent ourselves in any given situation. Most interesting of all, according to Goffman, not all of these moments or characteristics need to be factually accurate, nor true. Like comedians or actors who have gone full-method, we can improvise and fill in the empty beats with stories that will get us where we need to go, so long as we stay in character.

The year is 2006, Echo, soon-to-be 13 is in her first year of high school. Echo liked things that were black and music that was loud, Narcissus liked the same. Narcissus liked Slipknot and was influenced by his older brothers, now out of high school. Echo said she liked Slipknot, but only knew that one song about waiting and bleeding. Truthfully, Echo liked Panic! At The Disco, but that wasn't as cool as liking Slipknot. Slipknot was an acquired taste for the cultured children of the 8th grade. So Echo smiled and nodded, pretending to like the creepy-old-man music that haunted her dreams. Through this process of smiling and nodding, agreeing to like things she didn't quite enjoy nor understand, Echo metamorphosed into the personification of all things Narcissus liked.

Echo worked hard to mimic traits that Narcissus said he liked; Echo was outgoing, Echo was strong, Echo liked adventures,

Love

Echo could 'chillax' at the drop of a hat. Yet Narcissus chose someone else, time and time again, causing Echo to constantly recalibrate her personality. This year, however, with a larger pool of prospective romantic interests, Echo couldn't compete. The girls Narcissus dated had traits Echo couldn't mimic; they were popular, they were good at sport, they didn't have a curfew, they were allowed to drink at parties, they put out. The circumstances where Echo was excluded grew in number, there were no longer enough hours in the day to spend walking around the swampland with Narcissus, nor talk into the night, as he was doing these things, and more, with someone else. Echo retreated to the only other place she knew, her imagination, fuelled by the many wonders of a growing internet community.

With the power of a modem connection, Echo discovered MySpace, the platform that changed it all. It was on MySpace that Echo could experiment with her identity. MySpace meant that Echo didn't live in a small regional town isolated from the rest of the world. With just a few clicks Echo had found a connection to strangers and an entirely new universe of countercultures. Echo made a new identity, learning from the years of assimilation she had undergone to impress Narcissus. Echo made lists of things she really liked, without Narcissus Echo only had to impress, well, herself. Panic! At The Disco lead to My Chemical Romance which lead to The Used; favourite band rankings were a popular profile addition on MySpace and let others know which sub-genre she fit into. When Echo chatted to strangers on messenger the text under her screen name flashed with whatever song was playing on iTunes. Whenever Narcissus logged on Echo manually changed her status to 'Wait and Bleed - Slipknot', just in case he were to see. Though Slipknot was never downloaded from Limewire, just songs about not being ok and finding a box full of sharp objects. But Echo didn't want Narcissus to know what was really going on just from looking at an MSN now playing status; Echo wanted Narcissus to ask what was wrong.

George Herbert Mead, a social philosopher, believes that a distinguishing feature of human beings is our ability to imagine how others see us. We carry images in our heads not only of how we want to be perceived, but also of how others could be seeing us. This use of imagination is presumed to be distinctively human and helps us to construct our identities differently with the use of symbols. Our words, the pictures we take, the clothes we wear and how we wear them all symbolise something else entirely. A red dress, for example, serves the purpose of covering one's body, yes, but also could act as an indication of intention or mood; strength and passion. Further, language allows us to talk about things that are not in sight. We just discussed a red dress, perhaps one or both of us visualised a red dress, without the dress needing to be physically present. While culturally nuanced, these symbols transcend time and space with the aid of our imagination.

MySpace taught Echo many things; first that it was a numbers game. How many friends you had determined your popularity, and therefore symbolised your worth as a human being. Echo found new friends from all over the world and watched how they interacted, what they wrote and how they became *MySpace famous*. It started with pictures, taking lots of pictures. Echo learnt how to take a selfie, her Nokia now sporting a front camera that shot on at least two pixels. Echo soon moved on to using a digital camera, staging photoshoots in her room, in the gutter outside her house, at the shops and anywhere that looked good in black and white. Echo decorated her profile with images and posts, symbols if you like, that would attract friends with similar interests. Secondly, Echo learnt that what music taste one had dictated their personal style. It wasn't the runway that millennials looked to for fashion, it was the bands they listened to day in and out. Echo dyed her hair black, purchased hairspray and teased it up as high as it would go. A fringe in front and eyeliner for days, Echo was now part of the scene in her ratty converse and jumpers with thumbholes. This was Echo's first true identity, laden with social and cultural symbols in the form of clothing and accessories to let others know all her favourite things in the blink of an eye.

A few months into grade eight and Echo's MySpace friends list had grown to a few thousand. Echo posted bulletins with her innermost thoughts, feeling comfortable to be dark and gloomy; there were no consequences on the internet, and all the cool people 'felt really deep emotions, rawr xD'. Echo, for the first time in her life, felt true acceptance from a community; something she hadn't found within her family, neighbourhood or school. Echo wrote about family problems, feeling alone with no siblings or friends to spend time with, feeling rejection from Narcissus, her changing body and the angst of not knowing what direction she was headed in life. All Echo knew was that she loved music and words. She could manipulate both to tell stories and evoke emotions. The Internet was the perfect conduit for such a pursuit.

The third and final lesson that MySpace taught Echo was that there was no place on Earth her highschool frenemies couldn't go; there was no such thing as a safe place. A girl who liked Narcissus started a rumour, printed the pages from MySpace and distributed them around the school. The girl told everyone that Echo had a secret; Echo had intense feelings and listened to weird music on the internet. The rumour took over the campus, Echo was the last to know, finding out when students lined up at lunch to throw food at her, to laugh and point.

They called Echo *emo*, told Echo she had no friends, no one to love her. Echo was further excluded from friendship circles, not even the outcasts wanted her around, she attracted too much attention by just breathing. 'Why don't you go and kill yourself?' the crowd would jeer every day. Narcissus and his girlfriend watched on, standing in the shadow of the palm trees. 'I can't get involved,' Narcissus would say, 'it's important I stay neutral, y'know? Like Switzerland.'

Narcissus got a new best friend after that, the girl who started the rumour about Echo. Echo begged and pleaded with Narcissus, trying to explain the subtleties of manipulative girl-stuff. Narcissus grew tired of the drama that followed Echo like flies in summer. They went weeks on end without talking. Narcissus said 'sometimes it's ok to drift apart', staring off into the deep blue ocean behind the school. They didn't drift apart, not according to Echo, it was more like Narcissus lit Echo's raft on fire and shoved her out to sea on a stormy night, ignoring her cries for help.

The music Echo listened to started to take on new meaning, the lyrics explaining life experiences of people much older suddenly made much more sense. Each time Echo paid for a CD she was buying the feeling of love and acceptance from a male figure who wouldn't reject her. She was embraced by the words that were being screamed down headphones. Echo wished she could scream like that. Every time Echo went to write, went to talk about how she was feeling, nothing came out. Emotions trapped inside her chest; her heart would squeeze itself to death every day, contorting with every repressed sentence, every loss of autonomy.

Nowhere was safe. Echo was followed home from school like clockwork by tormenting packs of peers. MySpace was full of torments, reminders that Echo didn't fit in anywhere. Echo's life now revolved around music and getting to know the musicians who gave words to feelings beyond a 13-year-old's comprehension. Echo spent her time with her face glued to the computer screen, watching videos of musicians on tour, interviews about their hard-knock lives and how they made it big. Echo dreamed of meeting them, knowing they'd be instant friends, knowing that they'd not only accept Echo for being a little odd, but they'd appreciate Echo's insight and talent for wordplay. Echo had a safe place now, inside her mind with her beloved musicians for friends and family.

It was here that Echo continued to shape her identity, now

aligning it with a more adult-sized personality, the kind that could leave her backwards hometown and tour the world year in and out. The kind that everyone would love because Echo would make no mistake in how she was socially constructed. Echo would be the modern-day Juliet without the suicide, the contemporary Satine without tuberculosis. Echo would be swept off her feet by someone from another planet, most likely Los Angeles, and live the biggest romance narrative the world had ever seen. Even when The Used sung about drugs, bulimia and death, all Echo could see and hear was love, love, love. Each dollar Echo spent on music, on clothes, on books, was an investment in a better her. Each dollar Echo spent went towards buying love, the kind of love that couldn't say no, because it was the love that didn't know Echo existed.

It was music that carried Echo through the next five years, out and over the countryside to another state where no one knew Echo's story. Echo reinvented herself countless times throughout high school, adding new quirks and traits to her toolkit with each new song, movie, book; each friend made and each friend lost. Echo claimed the word *emo* until people stopped using it as an insult, Echo appropriated every other derogatory word until there were none left. When Echo left her hometown she didn't say goodbye to Narcissus, nor anyone else. Echo told no one that she left to find love, whether it be in a place, a space, a time, a thought, a song, a tree, a bird. But she left to find it. However, all Echo could find was Narcissus in different forms, a boy who had Narcissus' hair, a tree that looked like one they once sat under, someone who moved like Narcissus, someone who laughed like Narcissus. He was everywhere Echo went, he was in every face and every song, as if to haunt and torment, to punish Echo for leaving. He was Echo's first love and Echo couldn't escape.

Anthony Giddens writes that the rise of the shared romantic narrative has resulted in people constructing stories of their lives, their love affairs. This means that even if the relationships are to end, the story must go on. As already mentioned, Goffman writes the script needn't be true, nor fully based in reality, so long as the actors stay in character.

In 2011, Echo, now out of high school sans black hair, woke with a start in the middle of the night. There was a narrative she had been living, creating and telling for five years which had lasted longer than any semblance of a relationship with Narcissus ever had. Thousands of kilometres away Narcissus was calling out, Echo was sure of it, for that's what the story demanded. They hadn't spoken in years and Echo's heart ached with the distance, so Echo did what Echo did best. Echo wrote Narcissus a letter. For the first time, Echo told Narcissus how she felt, how much she loved him. The letter was posted before Echo could regret the countless soppy pages of romantic drivel. A week later Narcissus called, he wanted to meet up. Echo flew to him, heart in throat, ready to put it all on the line.

When Echo saw Narcissus he was older, hardened. His hair fell over his eyes like Romeo Capulet, his eyes sparkled like the ocean near where they walked. He had missed Echo, too. He wrapped Echo in the warmest embrace and whispered, 'I'm so happy you're here' until she squirmed away. They walked and talked for hours, dissecting where everything went wrong all those years ago. Narcissus, full of remorse, promised to never betray Echo again. Narcissus wanted to move to the east coast to be with Echo, to study marine biology at a top university. They could travel between semesters, ride their bikes around the country as they dreamed of doing as children. They agreed to be together no matter what. Serious, full of brevity. They were committed to being something, anything. Whatever it was they were going to do it together. Echo said 'I love you' as the sun set over the ocean. Narcissus said 'I'll say it when I see you next, when I move over east and we never have to be apart again'. Echo smiled, heart racing. She told herself that's just what Romeo would say. At long last, Echo's life was imitating art.

Love

Love was something Echo's life had revolved around since the turn of the century. Wanting a life full of romance, intrigue, adversity and triumph just like she had seen splashed across screens from a young age. Echo's first love started off child-like, innocent and carefree. It filled Echo with feelings of euphoria, wonder and elation; first love was hopeful and held infinite possibilities within an unknown future. As Echo grew up the love she had for Narcissus turned more serious, something she couldn't escape, nor wanted to. An emotional crutch, somewhere to turn despite Narcissus often not emotionally, nor physically, showing up. Echo simply filled the empty beats with her imagination. In her imagination, Narcissus was always there, and the story, like all great love narratives, went on. After trials and tribulations, countless people trying to keep them apart, Echo and Narcissus were going to set sail into the sunset, together forever.

To Echo, love was like a flower. It grows and blooms, it's beautiful, delicate and sturdy like a rose. You can't hold a flower too tight or else it crinkles and wilts away before its time. All you can do is let it rest on the palm of your hand and be grateful it's there while it lasts. To Echo, just like love, Narcissus was a flower, something she had admired but never truly possessed. After waiting for eleven years, Echo and Narcissus were blooming together; their love was a flower.

It was summer again when Echo got the call, she had been waiting for Narcissus to say he was coming, that the flights were booked. But the call wasn't from Narcissus, it was from someone else. They said Narcissus was in an accident. They said his heart stopped on the operating table at midday. They said Narcissus was gone and wasn't coming back.

Echo was right. Love is like a flower, and flowers die.

Limerence

I grew a flower that can't be bloomed in a dream that can't come true
—Fake Love, BTS

In fair Verona Beach, two star-crossed lovers are about to meet. The costumes scream 1990s, the vernacular is 1590 and everyone has a gun. Romeo Montague gatecrashes a Capulet party to see his love interest, Rosaline. He is not at all worried that the Montagues and Capulets are in a mafia blood war. While admiring fish in a tank that divides the male and female bathrooms, as they so often do, Romeo spies a singular green eye looking up at him, between the coral, from the other side of the tank. Though hundreds of litres of water separate them, to the human eye it looks like a thin veil of glass that keeps Romeo and Juliet apart. They stand and marvel at one another as fish swim past, swept up in a single moment where a world of romantic possibilities spread out before them. Just like that, they were in love, Romeo surely thinking 'Rosaline who?'. At this point, Juliet was dragged away to dance with Paris. Romeo chased after her and they held eye contact while she spun around the room with the astronaut man.

Echo had watched *Romeo and Juliet* countless times when growing up, enchanted by the use of old language with new technology and norms. The year was now 2019, Echo was 25 and sat in her room, watching Romeo discover Juliet through the fish tank, for the first time since her childhood. Each day Echo was absorbed by acts of nostalgia, like her emotional health was rooted in her ability to live in the past, replaying old scenes on repeat. In the years since Narcissus passed Echo had been busy adding more people, memories and places to the safe haven in her mind. In her youth, she used music to project her imagined self into the future. In her adult years, those old songs made up the soundtrack to the memories of people who were no longer hers. Images played in quick succession back-to-back like a retrospective montage. 'This is your life, Echo' says a smiling presenter to an audience of one.

What used to liberate Echo now trapped her in the room in her head, memories so badly warped she couldn't remember if they had been tampered with or not; if she had intentionally changed her childhood narrative to save face, or to stop the pain of remembering. Since Narcissus, Echo had been in love countless times. Each the same, she would spy someone across a room and could instantly see their shared future together. She would travel far into the future with them in the space of a few minutes before first words were ever exchanged. It was just like how Romeo felt when he first saw Juliet, Echo was sure of it. All it took was for the scene to show Romeo staring with *those* eyes at a demure Juliet and chasing after her to convey his feelings of love-at-first-sight. Surely it must be a universal feeling if no narration was needed to demonstrate that Romeo was besotted, entranced and felt like his heart would be wrenched from his chest if he couldn't have beautiful Juliet all to himself.

In the 1970s, experimental psychologist, Dorothy Tennov, interviewed her students on the topic of romantic love; the catalyst being two conversations she had that conveyed a particular kind of love, one with two male graduates and another with a female student.

Idol Limerence

After class one day Tennov listened to graduate students Fred and Bill describe their past relationships, where their breakups were so severe that they couldn't complete normal tasks. All they could manage was to be still and ruminate about their ex-girlfriends day in and out. This in itself was not what spurred Tennov to conduct research. It was a few weeks later when Tennov's student had come to request an extension, heartbroken from having been dumped by her fiancé via letter, that everything fell into place. The student noted not being able to think, not being able to do anything but lay in bed and think of her ex; all-consumed by the heartbreak.

Here, in the period of just a few weeks, Tennov had heard firsthand accounts of "an experience both extreme and banal, a pain whose source lay in completely uncharted regions of the human psyche" which were reported by both men and women. This is what made Tennov want to know if there was a definite series of universally experienced events that would lead to romantic love, despite the situations and circumstances differing vastly between individuals. Up until this point, Tennov thought her personal experiences of romantic love, which were similar to those her students reported, were unique to her. What she would soon discover was that they were indeed universal. This is how the phenomenon of limerence was first discovered, entering the world in the form of Tennov's 1979 book *Love and Limerence: The Experience of Being in Love.*

Forty years later, Echo was about to come to the same conclusion that Tennov and many others before her had; what she was experiencing wasn't just romance, nor heartbreak. Further, Echo was pretty sure she had lost all her marbles in the pursuit of love; a snide chorus of 'Echo is crazy. Echo is a stalker' haunted every corner of her consciousness.

Each time Echo thought about love she would feel something tug at her heart. A yearning for something, anything, that resembled love and acceptance. Cultural critic and intersectional feminist bell hooks writes that love heals, that people redeem themselves in the act and art of loving one another. When Echo looked back on her life of deeply loving so many people she could see that she was trying to heal. First by trying to heal from the absent love of Narcissus and, since 2011, trying to heal from the loss of Narcissus himself. Echo never got an 'I love you, too', yet still she searched for it in every person who had Narcissus eyes, smile, hands, hair or laugh, even if it meant her own demise. There was one other love that came close to Narcissus, though, perhaps the final nail in the coffin of Echo's love life. It was watching Romeo and Juliet that made his face float back to her. Usually, she would push it away. But the way Romeo chased after Juliet made Echo want to delve deeper into why she continued to run head first into the fire, ready to be hurt again.

On her first day of university in 2014, Echo sat in the back of the lecture theatre, her notebook and pen lying in wait for the class to begin. At 9:01 the lecturer was beginning to introduce themselves to the small cohort of students when *he* walked in.

He was tall, a blonde bowl cut parted across his broad forehead. He wore light blue jeans and a Joy Division tee, you know, the one with the waves on it that everyone has. He had Ray-Bans that still covered his eyes. His hightop converse were black and white, laced all the way up, with pristine bleached socks peeking from below his cuffed jeans. His bag was slung over one shoulder while he looked for a spare seat, sunglasses sliding down his nose as his eyes swept across the room.

Echo's nostrils flared at the sight of him.

He looks like a dick, she thought to herself.

Being late to the first day of classes was a criminal offence to her Type A personality. Echo prayed to the university gods that he wouldn't sit near her.

Three long strides up the stairs and he took a seat in the row below Echo's. He turned around, looking over his sunglasses while chewing gum. Their eyes caught, and he smiled. 100 watts right to Echo's heart. She recoiled. 'Jerk,' she muttered under her breath. It wasn't quite as captivating as Romeo, Juliet and the fish tank, but it was then that Echo fell in love with him. Felix.

In many ways, limerence can be understood as the feeling that comes before romantic love. Though it is debated whether or not limerence is a form of love, it most definitely is felt strongly. In fact, it is said to be the strongest of all emotions; but due to its inconsistent and often non-linear nature, it can be hard to measure. If Novak is correct when he writes that romance is a love for love itself, perhaps then it is limerence that precedes all else and is the result of a deep, all-consuming desire for love that has not yet been reciprocated.

According to Tennov, limerence has the following basic components: intrusive thinking about the limerent focus (originally termed the "Limerent Object" or "LO"); acute longing for reciprocation; fear of rejection and unsettling shyness in the presence of limerent focus; transient relief from intrusive thoughts through the fantasising of emotional reciprocation from limerent focus; intensification of feelings through adversity; a remarkable ability to emphasise what is truly admirable in the limerent focus, and; an ability to read into all actions of the limerent focus to analyse for potential emotional reciprocation.

'Get to know your classmates,' the lecturer called out at the end of the lesson, 'you'll be working closely with them for the rest of your degree. Directors, unless you're planning to write for yourself I suggest you find a writer and hold them close.'

Type-A-Echo had her bag packed and flew down the amphitheatre stairs as soon as the clock ticked to 10, on a mission to the library to bury herself in books.

She noticed Felix lazily reach for his bag as she breezed past and smirked.

Lord, let's hope he's not the director I get stuck with, she thought.

As she walked through the wide outdoor corridors that connected the campus buildings, Echo pondered the late boy's name, 'Felix', which he had so confidently declared to the room. She chuckled to herself, Felix the late boy and Felix the cartoon cat had identical shit-eating grins. The universe had a good sense of humour.

Echo paused outside the library to watch a kangaroo lazing in the sun, she remembered the kangaroos from her hometown and how they also spent a lot of time on the university campus there.

Perhaps, Echo mused, they are secret scholars who attain knowledge through osmosis while sunbaking.

Echo turned to the library and thought about Felix again.

I hope I don't attain his dickhead vibes through osmosis.

'Are you going up?' came a voice from beside Echo.

Echo jumped.

It was Felix.

Sunlight glinted off his hair as his fringe fell across his face. He bent his head down to grin at Echo while she stood with her mouth open, aghast.

His eyebrows rose, awaiting a response.

'No.'

Echo turned and walked towards the cafe on the other side of the grassy square.

Felix followed.

'Dr. P told me you were the last writer who hasn't elected a director to work with,' Felix took one stride for every three of Echo's, 'and I need a writer to work with.'

Echo paused, lips pursed.

'Why me?' she asked, glancing up at Felix, 'I mean, you could just write for yourself.'

Felix pointed to her maroon shirt that said *Ambush Reality*.

'Enter Shikari, right?' he smiled.

Echo's eyebrows rose.

'Joy Division, right?' she mimicked dryly, pointing at Felix's shirt.

'Ah,' his smile grew wider, 'you like them?'
Echo started walking again.
'Love, love will tear us apart, again.' She sang flatly, turning to look at him.
'They have other songs, you know.' Felix muttered.
Echo rolled her eyes.
'Sorry you're not a winner!' Felix shouted after her as the distance between them grew.
Echo whipped around, waiting for Felix to catch up.
'They have other songs, you know.' she grinned.
Felix laughed.
'Ok, how about *And I know that we've still got time, but I do not think we're invincible?*' he held his hands out in the air, waiting for Echo's approval.
Waiting.
Waiting.
Waiting.
'Ok, I'll write for you,' she sighed.
Felix made a fist and punched the sky, Breakfast Club style.
'Yes!' he exclaimed as they reached the cafe.
'Gotta go,' he winked, 'see you next week.'
And with that, he was gone.
'Not staying for coffee?' Echo whispered as she watched him stroll across the grass.
It was the intrusive thoughts that came first. The scene where they first spoke played on repeat day in and out. Echo collated all her favourite parts of Felix and played them like a movie trailer in her mind: his hair; his white socks; his cuffed jeans; his converse; his sunglasses; his stupid Joy Division tee. The way he bent his head down to look at her; the way he could walk as fast as her with half the effort; how his face lit up when he was excited; how he quoted her favourite lyrics as easily as breathing. Echo hated him so much, yet she couldn't stop thinking about every minute detail of their brief interaction.
He smiled at her.

He walked into the lecture theatre and sat right in front of her, then he smiled.

Their eyes met. They had shared an infinite lifetimes in that one glance, Echo was sure.

Echo was beginning to read into all of Felix's actions. She would analyse until she found the positive, until she found the real meaning hidden beneath the layers; he wanted her.

He could have opted to work alone, like many directors had, as there was a shortage of writers in their cohort. Instead, he had chased after Echo and pleaded with her to join him.

Well, it's not like Felix pleaded... He serenaded.

Yes, Echo thought, *that's more like it.*

Like how Romeo went to Juliet's window to call her out, to serenade her with his love.

Except Felix's presence was as unwelcome as the thoughts that swirled in Echo's mind.

Nothing a few shakes of the head couldn't fix.

One shake.

Two shakes.

Back to normal.

At the end of the first week Echo received a notification from her lecturer. She had an assignment, she had to write a scene and workshop it with her director. It had to be something personal, a life experience, an event, something unique to the writer.

Echo's heart suddenly constricted, twisted into a pretzel and beat so fast she thought she'd be sick.

He would read her work.

He, shit-eating Felix, would read her work, and soon.

What if he didn't like it?

What if he read Echo's writing and laughed?

What if he laughed so hard he fell off his chair?

What if he fell off his chair and then stood up and ran away from Echo?

What if he read Echo's writing and found her to be an unsuitable match?

'Er, this is awkward,' said the imaginary Felix in Echo's mind, sitting on the floor, just having fallen out of his chair, 'your writing is terrible and I don't think this is going to work out, you're kind of weird...' he quietly stands up and walks away, shaking his head in dismay.

What's not going to work out, though? Echo pondered.

What rejection was she more afraid of: the rejection of her work or the rejection of herself as a potential love interest? Another limerent trait: she was petrified of Felix not wanting her back.

Two clicks and Echo was on Felix's Facebook profile, scouring for hints, clues as to who he was and what he thought about the world. She viewed every photo, every status and every liked page she could find. She made a tally in her mind of the things Felix liked and compared them to what she liked. His taste in music was different, more advanced. While Echo liked five bands Felix liked fifty, and had a different song for every occasion imaginable. Each day he shared a video clip which conveyed a mood, an idea, a time and place perhaps only known to him and a few others. His wall had so many inside jokes shared between friends that Echo's head ached after the first ten minutes. But ten minutes was all she needed; she had deduced everything she needed to know about Felix.

After that ten minutes of lurking, her feelings had drastically shifted. Echo suddenly cared so much about what Felix thought. Although she had been confident in their first interaction she was now horribly shy. Hatred was replaced by the sheer terror of seeing him again, he was so cool. Echo had to step up her game, she had to be that level of cool in order to impress him.

'Impress him?' Echo whispered, 'why impress him? Who's idea was that?'

Echo looked around her bedroom.

'Impress him?' she said louder, clenching her fist, 'I want to destroy him!' she brought her fist down on her laptop.

Ah, shit, Echo thought, throwing herself backwards into her pillows, *now I'm really confused.*

Although Echo felt like these thoughts were not her own, she often found herself allowing them to wash over her. An active imagination meant she was able to construct narratives and ideas for her writing with ease. But with the looming deadline of producing a piece of work, she couldn't think of anything but Felix.

So Echo did what Echo did best, she took the qualities of Felix she found to be *almost* admirable and turned them into art. It was like the place she created these thoughts, these narratives and ideas, was a dreamscape.

A quiet garden in the dead of night, full moon peeking out from behind the clouds. Echo's ideas and feelings were seeds that she tended to, sometimes watering them every day, sometimes neglecting for weeks on end. Since Narcissus, these ideas and feelings were plants that took on many forms, rosemary, mugwort, sage; but never a flower. Through these fantasies that masqueraded as a creative process, Echo was able to find transient relief from her feelings of limerence; Echo felt sane.

The movie trailer that played in Echo's mind of all her favourite things: the socks; the hair; the smile, a familiar smile... like Narci- grew over the coming weeks with each fleeting interaction she had with Felix. She took a moment, a feeling, a glance, and channelled it into something new. She warped it, so he wouldn't know it was him she was describing in her stories.

So when he read her scene and said 'this person is a real dickhead' he was calling himself out. And when he smiled at the prose that not-so-coincidentally sat on the page next to the scene in her workbook, he was really smiling at the future Echo had imagined for them.

It was moments like those that gave Echo comfort in the first month of university, just an hour each week that she would spend with Felix. Every time he laughed or smiled at something she created she took it as an indication of his growing feelings towards her.

Conflicted, Echo only allowed herself to like him in moments of weakness. When she saw him in the flesh she became quiet, demure, unsure. When she looked at him she didn't know if she could like him. But when he was gone and not replying to her carefully crafted messages despite being online, her feelings grew along with her restless torment.

By the end of the fifth week, having spent just five hours in the company of Felix, Echo knew she had to do something more. Echo knew she had to make an excuse to see him every day. Without him, life was dull and meaningless. Her heart ached with each glance at the green glow of the *online now!* icon that sat next to his name on Facebook. She needed to give him a reason to write to her late at night and early in the morning; she wanted to be the one he posted ambiguous shoegaze songs about. After five weeks it had finally set in, what Echo had been feeling was an acute longing for emotional reciprocation from Felix; truthfully, at this point, she'd take whatever she could get. Slowly but surely, the seed in Echo's garden grew roots and started to peek out from the well-turned soil. This time, it was not rosemary, or mugwort, nor sage; it was a flower not yet bloomed.

'I have an idea,' whispered Echo to Felix while they huddled over a video camera in the dimly lit classroom.
'Mm,' Felix responded, adjusting the lens.
'Well, you know how we both like music and art,' Echo watched Felix's face as she spoke.
'Mm,' Felix pushed his hair back from his eyes.
'And how there's a lot of cool musicians you know,' Echo continued.
'Mm,' Felix straightened up to look at Echo.
'Well,' Echo said shyly, 'why don't we put on a show?'
'Go on...' the corners of Felix's mouth started to turn upwards.
'I was thinking we should have a business that puts on interactive art shows with live music,' Echo became more animated as she spoke, 'like we could project our short films onto the walls and have live art demonstrations while a punk band plays terri-

bly loud music in the middle of the room.'

Echo held her breath while Felix pondered her proposal.

'You know what?' Felix grinned, 'I love it!'

He picked Echo up and spun her around while they laughed.

Echo was euphoric, her heart was racing so fast she couldn't see straight. He wanted to work with her. He wanted to build a future with her. Suddenly a future where Echo was the one Felix would post songs about online became a very real possibility.

Over the coming weeks, Echo and Felix would meet every day before and after class to work on their business plan. They pooled their money and began to look for a venue; they would drive around listening to demos from local bands; they picked a business name and started to make promotional posters.

A month later Echo and Felix laid on a picnic rug while dreaming up their next short film.

They decided they wanted to film something different, a story where a girl likes a boy and wants to go to a party with him. He says he can't make it, so the girl goes alone and spies her love interest there with another. Heartbroken, she flees the party. Inevitably she stalks her love interest to the pine barrens where he takes this other girl... things deteriorate from there.

Echo and Felix planned out the entire film so that they could throw fake blood over everything in the forest that separated their region from the city. Neither was especially good at writing and directing horror, but both thought filming something spooky with their friends would be a whole lot of fun.

All Echo could think of was what it'd be like to travel to the pine barrens with Felix, what would happen in the dead of night. Though she was petrified of the dark all she could think of was romance; candles, wine, blankets.

Sure, it was a film set, but a girl could dream.

When Echo wasn't around Felix she was empty. When they weren't together it felt like she couldn't breathe. When she wasn't right in front of him he didn't talk to her, he didn't reply to messages and he didn't answer phone calls.

It was now May, a week out from filming the short film that Echo and Felix had vividly dreamed up.

Late one Saturday afternoon Echo got a message from Felix's friend, Cameron, saying he'll pick her up in a few minutes; they had an event to attend.

Why do you want to take me with you? Echo replied.

A surprise for Felix, Cameron wrote back, *he'll be stoked to see you.*

Echo's heart fluttered in her chest.

Stoked to see you flashed on the back of her eyelids each time she blinked.

They drove in silence down to the coast where houses as big as shopping malls lined man-made canals with boats parked out front.

Echo wore a dress, black and simple. The first dress she had worn in years.

She had spent every minute before Cameron arrived carefully pulling her hair back into a small bun. Not a hair out of place. She wore the faintest red lipstick and smelled ever so slightly of lavender.

'So what exactly is this?' Echo asked as she and Cameron approached the colossal front door to the mansion at the end of the street.

'Just some casual drinks,' he smiled, 'don't think too much of it.'

Echo held her breath as she walked into the marble hallway, water visible at the other end of the cavernous expanse through cathedral windows.

They wound their way throughout the house, Cameron had been here before.

Music sounded from the garden outside.

'We're here!' Cameron exclaimed, stepping out into the garden.

Felix was sprawled out on the grass, striped linen shorts and matching button-down shirt. His hair was longer and tussled.

He wore his Ray-Bans as he stared up into the sky.
Echo froze on the spot.
It wasn't dreamy Felix that made a chill go down her spine.
His head rested in the lap of another girl.
A slender, smiling, pale girl who smiled down at Felix as he pointed at clouds.
'Hey man,' Felix half-heartedly waved to Cameron.
'Look who I brought with me,' Cameron grabbed Echo by the wrist and pulled her out from the house.
Felix bolted upright.
The girl frowned at Echo, confused.
'Who is that?' she asked.
A beat.
A beat.
A beat.
Echo's stomach fell through the ground beneath her feet.
'Hattie, this is Echo,' Cameron positioned Echo in front of him, showing her off, 'she goes to university with Felix.'
Felix fumbled with the buttons on his shirt as he attempted to do them up to the top, until they nearly choked him.
Heat rose in Echo's cheeks.
'Oh, is she the girl you were telling me about?' Hattie asked Felix softly, intimately.
Felix ignored her.
'Oh, hi Echo,' he said, like he always did.
'Hi Felix,' Echo replied.

'I'm sorry,' said Cameron in the car on the way home at 7:45, 'I didn't know it was just those two. He's always had a thing for Hattie, I mean... have you seen her?'
Echo bit down on her lip.
What he surely meant was *have you seen you, Echo? You're not as perfect as Hattie.*
Later, as Echo stood looking at her reflection in the mirror, she counted all her flaws and listed them in her mind.

Idol Limerence

She returned to the garden where Felix rested his head on Hattie's lap. She stood herself next to Hattie in her mind, she compared her body to Hattie's. She took out a measuring tape and wrote down all the differences.

Hattie had a warm smile, Hattie's eyes were bright and brown, Hattie had perfect skin and expensive clothes.

Echo's smile was disjointed, goofy, odd. Her eyes changed from blue to green and back again, her mood plastered on her face for all to see. Echo's skin was strange, it didn't fit her well. Echo felt big and clumsy next to perfect, tiny Hattie. Echo felt like her stomach fat would fall out from her dress and drag along the ground. Echo didn't have expensive clothes or a nice house. But what upset Echo most of all was that Hattie had known Felix her entire life.

Echo couldn't measure up to Hattie.

Echo had sat awkwardly in the garden with Hattie and Felix and Cameron for hours, barely speaking, being her usual awkward self. Painfully aware that she was growing increasingly more unattractive with each passing, awkward, silent moment.

Hattie smiled and laughed and made conversation, Echo sat and stared at the water.

Worst of all, Echo knew she had to be ok with Felix's friendship with Hattie or else she'd come across as obsessive. Echo knew that to truly win Felix's affections she had to be as warm and nonchalant as Hattie was all evening.

'You're ok, aren't you?' Felix had chased after her as she left the house.

'Of course,' Echo smiled, 'I'm just tired, I've been writing something good for you.'

A lie.

'Oh yeah?' Felix looked down at his feet.

'Yeah, I might finish it later on,' Echo looked away, 'I have another party to go to after this.'

A lie.

'Oh yeah?' Felix said again, quieter this time.

'Yeah,' Echo summoned a big grin, 'I'll see you Monday.'

Echo crawled into bed. She didn't want to feel this way about Felix any more. Her heart broke into a thousand pieces that afternoon, and now as she lay in bed staring up at the ceiling all she could think of was how much she loved him.

Somehow, the challenge of Hattie being close with Felix made Echo want him more; her feelings grew through adversity. Though many signs could be interpreted as Felix being disinterested in her, she knew he wasn't.

Would he have chased after her as she left with Cameron if he didn't like her? Would he have agreed to establish a creative enterprise with her if he didn't want her around all the time?

Echo played happy scenes with Felix in her mind until she drifted off to sleep.

Perhaps, she thought, *I just need to show him that I'm more committed than Hattie. I'll win over his friends first.*

May passed by quickly. The launch of their business was set for June 25, the first day of the semester break. They had booked bands, hired a venue and started a lengthy social media campaign to get every young person in the area to show up. Campus was buzzing with excitement as other students offered to help out, donating supplies and creating new artworks for the event.

Echo and Felix invited their friends around to Echo's house at the end of the month to film the party scene, they decided it would be Echo that Felix would flirt with. Echo begrudgingly agreed to let Hattie play the stalker girl who would inevitably attempt to murder her in the pine barrens. Echo sought a kind of comfort knowing she would soon have footage of Hattie being a creepy stalker. But that was not the scene she played on repeat in her darkened room as winter grew cooler.

Under purple stage lights, Echo sat with Felix on a couch at their faux party surrounded by their friends. While Felix pretended to flirt with Echo, Echo didn't have to act at all. She smiled and looked at Felix in awe. It was this scene that she rewatched time and again. They danced at the end, once they had the footage they needed. Not a slow dance, nothing aesthetically pleasing. They just jumped around and pulled faces at the camera. Echo watched this every day until the image of them happy together was burned into her eyes.

Each day Echo made a concerted effort to face Felix with a smile, determined to show herself as happy and carefree. She wanted to be detached enough that he would want to keep her around, she wanted to be laid back so he would continue to take her everywhere. To bars, to clubs, to gigs, anywhere that the cool kids went Felix would follow, camera in hand. Echo believed him to be the tastemaker for anyone under 30, his networks and friendship circle soon became Echo's by association. For the first time in her life she had friends, or at least the semblance of them.

'Do you think he likes me?' Echo asked Cameron one day in June.

'Who, Felix?' Cameron laughed, 'I don't know, I keep asking but he won't tell me.'

'You think I'm alright, though, right?' Echo joked.

Cameron shot her a look.

Echo looked away.

'You coming to the Hampton party on Saturday?' Cameron changed the subject.

'Hampton Party?'

'Yeah, it's just down the road from your house. Ask Felix to pick you up, get him drunk... he'll spill his guts.'

The next day Echo and Felix were driving to university.

Felix picked up Echo each day now despite her house not being within a reasonable detour of the campus. He drove an extra twenty minutes to her house, just to see her.

She thought about that a lot.

'I just realised,' Felix fiddled with the buttons on the dash, 'that we don't have a song.'

Echo's heart fluttered.

'What?' she knew what.

'You know, a song just for us.'

'Oh, like on The O.C.?' she laughed.

'Yeah, but it's not going to be Forever Young,' Felix grinned.

He pressed play on his phone, one hand on the steering wheel, no eyes on the road.

Bubblegum pop filled the car.

Echo's eyes grew wide.

'Is this Architecture in Helsinki?'

Felix nodded.

'It sure is.'

'I love it.'

They bobbed their heads along to their song while they drove the back streets to class.

'Hey…' Echo turned the volume down as the song ended, 'do you wanna go to the party at the Hampton's on Saturday with me?'

Felix turned into a parking spot.

'Hmm,' he said aloud, 'I don't think I can make it.'

'Oh,' Echo felt her cheeks go red, 'ok then.'

It was Saturday night, the cold winter air made Echo's bones ache as she stood outside the Hampton's house. She was dressed in black jeans and a jumper, the collar of her blouse sitting over the top studded with small gold pins. She had a bad feeling about this, but figured it was better to be seen at the so-called party of the year than not.

The entire Two Door Cinema Club discography played on repeat as Echo walked down the side of the house to the tiered garden below. Floodlights shone up from the orchard beyond with blinding hot whiteness that couldn't be blinked away, casting tall eerie shadows that moved with the breeze.

Echo stood on the top of the stairs and looked down at shadows of all the people she didn't know spread out in varying forms of disarray.

A hand appeared in front of her face holding a plastic cup, the red kind Echo often saw on U.S. television shows.

Idol Limerence

'Death punch!' shouted Cameron.

'Wha-'

'Shh,' Cameron sidled up to Echo, drinking from his own cup, 'don't think just drink.'

'Words to live by,' Echo muttered, pinching her nose as she threw back the purple-black concoction.

'You didn't come with Felix?' Cameron slung an arm around Echo.

'Nope,' Echo stared into the bottom of her empty cup.

'Ah,' Cameron swayed from side to side, 'that sucks.'

'Yep,' Echo looked around for more alcohol.

The music grew louder and the crowd swelled, more and more people pushing past them en route to the orchard below. Cameron steered Echo towards a lower level, out of the way of the blond-haired surfer guys who kept jostling her as they walked by.

Echo was dizzy, swearing off alcohol after her second cup of death punch.

Cameron was standing closer than normal, but Echo was too drunk to even open her mouth. Her plan was to stand still until she sobered up then walk home through the forest. Not her best plan, not her worst. She felt like living dangerously, precariously; maybe if she needed rescuing Felix would show up just in time. Maybe that's how she could get him to care.

'What should I do?' Echo thought aloud.

'What?' Cameron shouted over the top of the music.

Echo bit her lip.

'How do I get him to like me back?'

Cameron nodded his head absentmindedly.

'You could try making him jealous?'

'What do you mean?'

'You could just get with someone else, like how Felix is spending all his time with Hattie. That's driving you mad, right?'

Echo pondered for a split second.

'Yeah, it feels like I'm no longer sane,' she laughed to herself.

Cameron turned to face Echo, his eyes travelling to the left of her head as the music changed again.

'What?' Echo started to turn her head to see what Cameron was looking at.

Before she could blink Cameron placed one hand on the side of her face and dragged her towards him.

Wet lips pushed onto hers.

Echo felt sick.

She thought if she pulled away she might tumble down the hill.

The crowd below cheered as the music stopped, all eyes were on Cameron and Echo.

Echo took a step backwards, dazed and confused.

The cheers from the crowd quickly changed into a collective 'ah,' as they inhaled sharply, pained faces.

They all turned back to what they were doing before Cameron kissed Echo, Two Door blasting from the rooftop once again.

Echo turned around, the hairs on the back of her neck standing high.

There, on the step above was Felix and Hattie holding hands.

Felix looked as pale as a ghost.

Hattie looked like she could have her cake and eat it too.

She had a smile so broad it was about to fall off her face.

The same shit-eating smile Felix had, just not tonight.

Echo's world spun out of control as she felt her pulse beat through her eyeballs.

She was too drunk for this, she was definitely too drunk.

Felix let go of Hattie's hand and turned on his heel, walking back towards the road.

'Felix...' Echo called out softly.

She went to chase after him.

Cameron held her back.

'Stop it,' Echo said, teeth clenched, 'don't touch me.'

Cameron pulled her closer.

'Cameron!' Echo shouted, 'let me go!'

The orchard fell silent again as everyone stared at Cameron and Echo.

Cameron's face flushed red.

Above them, Hattie laughed to herself, pupils tiny in the blinding light.

Echo didn't see Felix in the week leading up to the show. She avoided him, heart racing every time she caught a glimpse of hair that might be his out of the corner of her eye. He was avoiding her, too. Instead of going to class Echo watched the live stream lecture from home. They exchanged cordial texts about run times and invoice payments.

Suddenly, Echo wasn't invited to gigs or parties. She was back on the outside where she started at the beginning of the year.

Felix said he'd cut the short film and rig the projectors for the event.

All Echo had to do was show up and play hostess.

Echo got a haircut and a new dress. Echo found all her old school friends and convinced them to come to the show. They were confused as to why she was suddenly talking to them again; they weren't as cool as Felix and his crew of mismatched renegades. Though, her friends noted, they were more upper-middle-class masquerading as renegades; that wasn't very punk.

Echo let her friends make snide remarks about Felix, she tallied all the things she disliked about him in her mind in the hope it would make her like him less.

Each time she thought about his smile, she would picture how he looked on the first day of class; how he sometimes got acne near his lips; how he was underweight; how he was going prematurely bald. Sometimes she had to distort her memories, but sometimes she didn't.

Echo was conflicted, when she didn't see him she thought she'd be ok. She didn't like him half as much. She didn't yearn for reciprocation.

But when she saw Felix dancing in the front row at their show

Limerence

with Hattie her heart broke all over again.

Her heart broke again when their films from the semester just gone played on the walls, covering the audience with their memories. Memories now so distant she thought perhaps they were made up. Maybe it was all for show, maybe what she thought Felix felt towards her was just him acting in front of the camera.

Were they even friends?

When the last band played Echo's world stood still when their final project played on the wall. The scenes they had filmed in her house were warped, different. They were cut in a way that made Echo look like she was stalking Hattie. New scenes were added, Cameron was on-screen speaking with subtitles.

She made me kiss her, he spoke into the camera, *she wanted to be Hattie but she couldn't get Felix to love her back.*

Test shots from the pine barrens of Echo staring through trees at Felix's parked car were used to illustrate just how far she'd go to get her man. The dance scene from the house party showed Echo dancing while she stared at a disinterested Felix.

Was that really what happened?

Were her memories really that twisted?

Echo's friends laughed at the mockumentary, not knowing that the only person it mocked was her.

Across the other side of the room stood Felix.

They were separated by a sea of moving bodies entranced by the band, blissfully unaware of the film projected to their left.

The crowd moved like the ocean, in huge waves they jumped up and down, Felix's face swimming in and out of view. The film froze on a still of Echo's goofy smile; a shot from the day she asked Felix to start a business with her. One of the happiest and hope-filled of her life.

Echo pushed past her friends and stumbled out into the cold night.

Inside, Felix turned back to Hattie, and the show went on.

The only thing to end the to-be relationship was the end of her life as she knew it; she and Felix never spoke again after that night. He transferred out of next semester's classes which they had feverishly enrolled in to remain together for the rest of their four-year degree. Echo didn't see him around anymore. What she did see, though, was their short film being shared amongst their mutual friends on Facebook. What she saw was how they called her crazy, how they said she forced Cameron to kiss her to get back at Felix for dating Hattie. How she brought new clothes and got a haircut to emulate the perfect Hattie. How she manipulated Felix into working all semester with her as part of a plot to make him fall in love. How Felix woke up to her games just in time, with the generous help of Hattie and Cameron, of course. Screenshots of her goofy smile were shared far and wide, she was the biggest meme of their film cohort for that year.

The flower that she had grown for Felix never bloomed, but failed to die. When Narcissus died so did his flower, but Felix's lived on. No matter how hurt she was, no matter how much she hacked at the stem, it didn't budge. Some days she hated him, others she loved him. Often she would wake up in the middle of the night positive he was calling to her.

One night in spring Echo burned the remains of the garden in her mind; not just Felix, but every other memory she had made went up in flames. She had grown a flower that could not bloom, in a dream that couldn't come true.

It wasn't until that night in 2019 that it all fell into place for Echo as she typed search words into her phone, diagnosing her past relationships. It wasn't love that she had experienced with Felix, but limerence, a word which she had found on a deep dive of obsessive-love research. She had a feeling she had been limerent her whole life; somehow learning how to categorise and analyse it made her feel slightly better. It made the pangs of heartache and guilt she felt when she thought of Felix disappear into the background.

Echo said goodbye to Romeo and discarded her laptop in the depths of her blankets. She moved throughout her room, throwing outfits over her head as she sought out something truly villainous. Sick of retrospectives, she was going to go out and see some friends. She was never going to think of Felix again, something she had been telling herself for the past five years. Ten minutes later and she was on the road, weaving between streets to get to the notorious shared house that sat near the beach: The Pound. Its inhabitants were indeed a pack of self-proclaimed dogs, Echo spent time with them so that she could stop thinking. To focus on the pointless drunken ramblings of 20-somethings who chain smoke and dance like it's still the 70s made her feel like her life wasn't so bad.

By the time Echo arrived the party was in full swing. What exactly the party was for was anyone's guess. Echo decided it could be a party for her new 'I don't give a fuck about boys' attitude. She figured that was more than worthy of celebration.

Echo was dressed all in red, the tightest dress she could find that sat above her knee; red earrings that dangled and swayed as she walked, and impossibly tall red heels. Echo decided that 2019 was going to be the year of red and she was leaning in, hard.

The Horrors', *I Can't Control Myself*, was blasting through the hallways of the house as people spilled out into the back yard. Echo hadn't heard that song in years.

She wove her way between bodies and bottles. Some people heard her footsteps and turned their heads so fast their necks nearly snapped; some people jumped out of her way. There was tension in the air. By the time Echo reached the grand room of the house, bordered by sweeping staircases, the energy was palpable. Something was about to happen.

Echo rolled her eyes, it was probably another knife fight.

"My Queen!" came a booming voice from atop the stairs.

The crowd parted and a scraggly haired man appeared.

Tight jeans, no shirt and a billowing robe that hit on everyone as he bounded down the staircase.

"Well, if it isn't Julian Casablancas himself," Echo said coolly.

"Naw, doll, don't call me that, he's not cool anymore," Julian Casablancas wrapped an arm around Echo and kissed her on the side of the head.

"What's with the party? I don't know half these people," Echo looked around the room, strange faces staring back at her.

Julian looked around, lost in thought.

"Echo, when are we going to write that book?"

"What book?"

"The book about *her*, you know who I mean, the love of my life," Julian swayed to the music, still holding Echo.

"The young girl from five years ago you keep talking to me about?"

Julian nodded enthusiastically.

Echo paused, looking up into the face of her old friend.

"How are you so sure it's love?"

Julian sighed.

"Because I can't stop thinking about her. Every song I write is about her. Everything I see makes me think of her beauty. We have run away together a thousand times and I have kissed her a thousand more."

"Oh," Echo nodded, "but I thought you've never kissed her?"

"Mm," Julian closed his eyes, "only in my dreams."

"Have you ever heard of limerence?" Echo asked softly, barely audible over the hum of the crowd.

"Limerence?" Julian shouted.

"Yeah," Echo shouted back, "like when you can't stop thinking about someone and your thoughts are out of your control and your heart aches for them and you're certain it's the greatest love story ever told?"

Julian straightened up, letting go of Echo.

"Oh like you and—" He cut his words off, looking to the side of the room.

Echo followed his line of sight, but saw nothing of interest.

"Felix?" she said softly.

"Yeah, the black cat, you had it bad for him," Julian shouted as the music grew louder.

"In my defence, I'm pretty sure he had it bad for me," Echo shouted back.

The music cut out.

"I thought Felix and I were going to be together forever!" Echo shouted.

The room went silent, all eyes on her.

Julian's eyes grew wide as he looked over Echo's shoulder.

Echo's stomach fell.

The music that was playing before was all-too familiar.

It had been tugging at the corners of her memories.

The crowd, the celebration, Julian anxiously scanning the room when he thought Echo wasn't looking. It could mean only one thing.

Echo slowly turned around.

It was him.

Felix.

He stared at Echo, expressionless. His posse fanned out behind him in formation, like they had been waiting for this moment all night.

Felix was taller, wearing black Doc Martens, black jeans, a black shirt and a black jacket. His hair was longer, his eyes were darker, it looked like he had been trying to grow a beard with little luck. His jaw was rigid, no shit-eating smile in sight.

A pale hand wrapped itself around Felix's shoulder.

"Hi Echo," a familiar voice came from behind Felix.

A girl Echo's height stepped out from the shadows, resting her head on Felix's arm while she held him.

Echo took a step backwards, recoiling as she pieced together fragmented memories in her mind. She rushed about her nighttime garden, turning over the soil in the hope she could find where she buried the pieces of paper. The paper she had written all her thoughts upon, all the detailed accounts of her days at university with Felix. All the car rides and dances by moonlight;

every moment shared and lost. She had tried to throw them away but couldn't, yet now when she needed them most they were nowhere to be found.

"Felix just graduated with his PhD, you know," the girl purred, "so we flew back from Melbourne for a little..." she paused, "hurrah," she laughed.

Echo's nostrils flared.

"Should've known you were coming," she walked towards Echo, "you just can't stay away from him, can you?"

"Hattie," Julian groaned, "don't be a bitch."

Hattie stopped in front of Echo, blinking coyly.

"And to my surprise, not only are you here, but you're still harping on about how much Felix loved you," she laughed again, looking at Felix.

"Yet Felix says you forced yourself onto him and he didn't know what else to do but be kind to the class weirdo," she slid a glance back towards Echo.

The posse snickered.

"Poor, lonely Echo is making up stories again," Hattie walked back to Felix, draping an arm around him, "aren't you glad I saved you from her all those years ago?"

Echo rolled her eyes. On the outside she was calm and composed.

On this inside, her heartbeat built in her chest.

She had to do something before she started crying.

Her throat constricted.

She had to leave.

Fast.

"Flattie," she looked at Hattie, "Felix," she looked at Felix, "I'm done."

Hattie's eyebrows rose.

"What?" she spat.

Echo shrugged.

"I'm just... done with this," Echo waved her arms around the room, "your intellectual imperialism is gross and I frankly

Limerence

couldn't care less."

Felix's nostrils flared.

Echo's chest swelled as she clapped her hands together excitedly.

"I'm free!" she exclaimed to no one in particular.

She looked Hattie dead in the eye.

"Thank you so much," she held her hands over her heart, "I truly mean it."

A lie.

With that, she was gone; she never saw Hattie and Felix again.

Echo cried all the way home, skipping through music because no song felt right. She felt foolish for having come across like she wasn't over Felix. But, truthfully, maybe she wasn't. Her heart had stung when she saw him. Jealousy nearly devoured her whole when Hattie appeared, arm so casually draped about Felix's shoulders.

"You're too old to be feeling like this," Echo muttered as she turned the car onto her street.

Though it hurt, she had felt liberated when she saw Hattie and Felix at the party. Echo was pleased to know they were still living in the past and very much still thought of her. But now she mourned the loss of a love she thought would live forever. First Narcissus, then Felix, she couldn't seem to separate the two. Both were fates that were out of her control.

Up the stairs to her house she stomped, shoes long discarded in the back of her car.

Echo lay in bed and tried to watch the rest of Romeo and Juliet, but it didn't feel right. She knew they were doomed, she didn't want to watch them die.

Frustrated, Echo turned to YouTube, letting the algorithm take her on a journey through time and space, one music video at a time.

Echo's thoughts moved from Narcissus to Felix to the slew of meaningless relationships she gave herself to since. She wrote all the criteria of limerence as a list in her mind and evaluated every person she ever loved; trying to find answers, trying to diagnose herself. Echo thought that if love was a flower then limerence was a dream, a dream of a flower in bloom. Further, this limerence, this dream, was a garden. The flower needed it in order to take root and flourish. Echo realised perhaps she needed limerence. Every story, every scene, every poem she had ever written was borne of limerence. If all she had was love she wouldn't have enough to write about, without yearning for reciprocation there was no tension. Without heartbreak, there was no story.

Echo thought back to The Pound that night and how empowered she felt to know that Felix and Hattie had seen her living her best life. All in red and turning heads; she was happy at that moment. In the years after Felix, she had thrown herself into conscious self-creation, she realised she had built her identity and life around Felix. So when he left she was destabilised, lost and confused. Tonight had affirmed that she was on the right track, but perhaps there was one final step. Instead of rejecting her younger self that was so harshly burned by Felix and his friends, she needed to hold her close. She had to find a way to balance her past, present and future selves. And most of all, she had to love herself wholeheartedly. For who else could love her if the best she could do was stand in the mirror and list all her flaws?

YouTube had taken her down a rabbit hole, she had started on nostalgic music that reminded her of Felix, but now she didn't know where she was.

The screen before her was white, the words *Big Hit* written large.

"What?" she said aloud.

No one answered.

Her finger hovered over the home button while she decided whether to let the video play or not.

The sound of a horn or a trumpet or something she couldn't quite name sounded. Slow, alluring. Maybe she was fragile, vulnerable or drunk. Maybe she was feeling anarchic. She let it play despite not being able to make sense of the video title.

BTS (방탄소년단) she read over and over.

"What is this?" she asked aloud again.

The clip opened on seven men sitting at a table, whether they were all the same person or not, Echo couldn't tell.

They kind of all looked the same.

They wore bright suits with patterns that clashed.

One minute they were sitting.

And then, suddenly, they all...

Started dancing.

Echo looked away and squelched a giggle.

"What are they doing?"

She looked back at the screen, now transfixed.

Someone with blue hair started rapping, half in English and half in something else; Echo couldn't tell what. He was familiar, something tugging at the back of her memories, but she couldn't place it.

She moved closer to the screen.

With each passing beat, she moved closer and closer still until she could barely see the screen. 3 minutes and 51 seconds passed in the blink of an eye.

"I think I hate it," Echo whispered to herself, unsure of exactly where in the universe she was just transported, "no wait..."

She frowned, thinking.

"Actually," she played the video again, "I think I love it."

That night while she waited to fall asleep she thought of that technicolour music video. She replayed shots over and over. She liked the way it made her feel.

Ah, she thought as she closed her eyes, *all of a sudden it feels like anything is possible.*

While she slept, unbeknown to her, the garden in her mind began to rebuild.

Like a phoenix from the ashes, limerence rose again.

Idol

So only above the surface of the water do I breathe, and the interest in me ends
—Whalien 52, BTS

Ballerinas sit on the floor of a New York studio while a pianist in the corner plays Tchaikovsky. 28-year-old Nina Sayers, dressed in white, dances before them as she auditions for the lead role in *Swan Lake*. She finishes and looks to the director expectantly; hesitant, waiting as he strides to her. Nina had not shown him the Black Swan, her darkness. She must dance again to fight for the role.

'Not so controlled,' the director shouts as she dances.
'Seduce us.'
'Not just the prince but the court.'
'The audience.'
'The entire world.'
'Come on!' he continues to shout as she dances.
'Attack it, attack it,' he snaps his fingers.

As Nina continues to turn she watches the directors face fall in bitter disappointment. She had failed to embody the Black Swan.

Echo watched *Black Swan* when it was first released in 2010, transfixed by the process Nina underwent to become a performer. The pain, the sacrifice, the failure. She loved to see how Nina had to embrace her darker side, how she lost touch with reality in the process; there was something both real and poetic about it. This was how a star was born, this was the eternal struggle of a performer, needing to be both white and black swans. To not be so controlled, to seduce the audience and all those around them, they had to become someone entirely new to achieve their dreams while remaining themselves. A contradiction, a complexity, a torturous fate; that is what Echo loved about Black Swan.

The morning after Echo watched the music video for *Idol* she woke with a start, a feeling of impending doom settling over her body. It was as if the day had started without her and she was late to catch up; with who or what remained unknown. She worked from home after all and there was no real reason to be awake at 4am. Echo's ears rang like she had been up all night. She felt as if she'd had a thousand conversations in her sleep and travelled halfway around the world. Her heart was racing like she had just seen a ghost.

Echo had forgotten all about BTS until she found herself back at her laptop. It was as if she blinked and was standing at the kitchen table with her eyes glued to the screen. Another BTS video before her, Echo didn't remember searching for it. But now that she thought of it she would like to watch that music video again, wherever it took her inside her own head was a nice place. She still felt fragile from seeing Felix. She needed an escape.

This music video wasn't the one she had seen the night before, though. She frowned at the unfamiliar start and the eerie whistling before the music began. This wasn't the BTS she remembered; although she had only seen them for just under eight minutes the night before, she felt as if she knew them deeply. As she watched the music video for *DNA* she tried to figure out who was who, unsure if these seven young men were the same as the ones from *Idol*. They were younger, their hair was different, everything had changed.

Echo looked around the kitchen as if she were about to be sprung watching a BTS video. She could see they were popular, *DNA* had hundreds of millions of views. She'd never seen a video with so many before. Somehow she felt guilty for watching, guilty for enjoying something so commercial.

What would Felix think? She thought.

"Fuck Felix," she said aloud, leaning in to see BTS better.

Though they kept changing outfits with each set, by the end of the video Echo started to recognise who was who. Some were rapping, some were singing and they all danced. She'd never seen anything quite like it. Half of her wanted to laugh but the other half wanted to take them seriously. Transfixed, she sought out more videos to satiate her growing curiosity.

What she didn't quite know at this moment was that she was beginning to interact with an idol group, and not just any idol group. One that would change her life forever. Seeing these seven young men living their dreams on the world's stage made Echo curious as to what her dreams were. If she could be in the position of BTS, with the influence and power, what would she do?

BTS, an acronym for 방탄소년단 Bangtan Sonyeondan, in English, Bulletproof Boyscouts, are a seven-member group hailing from South Korea. Echo thought it was funny that BTS had as many members as Voldemort had Horcruxes, in a way when she first saw them she believed them to be fragments of her soul. She joked to herself that perhaps that made her Voldemort. By the end of the day she knew each of their names, there was 김남준 Kim Namjoon, RM; 김석진 Kim Seokjin, Jin; 민윤기 Min Yoongi, Suga; 정호석 Jung Hoseok, j-hope; 박지민 Park Jimin, Jimin; 김태형 Kim Taehyung, V, and; 전정국 Jeon Jungkook, Jung Kook. As she studied their faces she couldn't decide who to focus on first, or most; there was so much beauty

Idol

to take in. It felt like the horizons of her mind broadened with each exchange of eye contact between her and the screen.

"I think I love them," Echo whispered as she pressed play on yet another music video.

Bitter memories of Felix washed away each time Echo's eyes rapidly moved about the screen, trying to keep up with BTS' choreography. The colours were so bright that they reached through the internet and wrapped around her brain.

Echo blinked and she was back riding her bike with Narcissus, they laughed and played on tree-lined streets while the sun set over the ocean. Watching a BTS music video reminded Echo of the euphoric feeling she would get opening presents at Christmas. Bright yellows and reds and blues, the flashing lights on the trees and the warmth of celebration. These memories were not her own; BTS made Echo nostalgic for a childhood she never had.

Each time Echo reached for her laptop in the early morning she couldn't help but learn more about them. She learnt all their likes and dislikes, their star signs, their heights. Echo tried to stop herself, but only half-heartedly; she was having too much fun. She felt like all this information on BTS was laid out just for her, each question that popped into her head was answered with a few clatters of keys. *Blink, blink,* Echo downloaded information from the internet into neatly categorised mind-piles at the speed of light. Her brain was a sponge made just for pointless BTS facts; she didn't need to know how tall they were, or what qualities they found attractive in women. But now she cherished these brightly coloured mind-piles like she did books stacked high on her desk. Knowledge was fun, especially when it was about unattainable boys in blouses.

"And to think I'm nearly 26 years old," Echo mused to no one in particular.

BTS had walked the same path as many South Korean groups had before them. These groups exist within the realms of

Idol Limerence

K-pop (Korean Pop), a term used for a diverse and often hard to define grouping of musicians and musical acts that originate from South Korea. According to Aja Romano in a 2018 Vox article, K-pop is a "distinctive blend of addictive melodies, slick choreography and production values, and an endless parade of attractive South Korean performers". K-pop is often regarded as mass-made pop-music drivel by the envious West, but K-pop is far more than that.

According to Yoongi during a 2018 interview at the Grammy Museum, K-pop is the integration of music, fashion, makeup and choreography that, when combined, become a kind of audio-visual package. This analogy of K-pop can be taken further when the work of BTS is closely examined to include the kinds of sweeping narratives one would usually see in movie trilogies; staging to rival a dramatic interpretation of Shakespeare at the Opera House, and a message for mass social change that transcends cultural and language barriers like a Live Aid concert. In many ways, K-pop is the curated amalgamation of cultural movements and methods, both Eastern and Western, that have shaped the world since the rise of mass media.

Nothing exemplifies the power of the K-pop industry, nor the vision of South Korea as a fledgling, yet powerful, nation borne of an ancient culture, quite like BTS. Aja Romano goes on to write that it's best not to ask what makes a song K-pop, rather what makes a K-pop performer. This chapter, instead of delving into what defines a K-pop song or group, will explore and analyse what makes an idol, for an idol is what sells the song itself and sets K-pop apart from other music genres. This is also not to make claims that BTS are only a K-pop group, such a statement tends to be controversial in current times. Perhaps as they continue to be fluid and hard to define. Rather, this book aims to show that BTS sit within a K-pop context which needs to be understood to better understand the group themselves.

In the broad and complex landscape of K-pop, those who prepare as trainees and debut as rookies in South Korea, if successful, go on to become idols. The success of an idol, or an idol group, is contingent on their ability to create, foster and build a devoted fan base. In other words, what separates idols and musicians is the size and dedication of their respective fanbases. In the years between the formation of BTS in 2010 and their debut in 2013, members were auditioned or scouted and trained in a range of creative and professional areas. This is a typical progression for idol groups; members must take lessons in singing, rapping and dancing, that's a given. But perhaps where K-pop diverges from Western music is in the tried-and-true methods of building the identities and fan groups of the future idols.

Sure, in the West it is common for celebrities to undergo lessons in speech, perhaps they learn how to pose for a red carpet, or maybe they get training for those pesky media interviews so they can dodge unwanted questions with a smile and a laugh. But the training is inconsistent across the board, perhaps the individual sought training of their own volition, perhaps they did it to take on a more desirable accent at the direction of their agency, it differs from case to case.

However, no one does it quite like South Korea, where the founder of SM Entertainment, 이수만 Lee Sooman, coined the term *cultural technology* to refer to the way in which Korean pop culture, or Korean wave, was, and still is, promoted globally. This cultural technology was originally disseminated in the form of a K-pop manual, providing a guide for the stages of casting, training, producing, marketing and managing which all staff members of SM Entertainment were instructed to learn. These stages remain present in the strategies of entertainment companies in South Korea to this day.

Echo spent her time that week split between exploring the technicolour landscapes of BTS' music videos and exploring her own prejudices. The second she started to enjoy BTS she was overcome with feelings of unease, like she was doing something that stood in opposition to her own morality. You see, when she found BTS and felt her heart leap from her chest, she connected with them as humans, as equals. Yet the more she learnt of them, the larger the gap grew between where she stood, as a 25-year-old arts producer in a small town, and where they stood, on the world's stage.

In her mind, she had constructed a narrative for how music needed to be made for it to be good, a narrative which she had been carrying since her early teens when she would lay and listen to angst-ridden music deemed alternative for days on end. BTS, from where she saw them now, didn't fit with this picture of a struggling musician. They were affluent, successful, and most of all, they were mass-made. As in, they were made for the masses with care and precision. This is the first issue Echo faced, she was conflicted about how to feel about the group. Which brings us to the first defining feature of an idol: they are both loved by their fans, and hated by their competitors and the general public who remain unaffected by an idol's charms.

It's all too easy to shun popular music or popular acts. For liking what everyone else does, what young women like, isn't the *in* thing. Music for the masses is, more often than not, mass-produced. This leads people to assume it is of lesser quality, has less of a message and meaning. If it's mass-produced then surely it can't be organic, it can't be real music. Further, an idol is selling more than just music. They're selling themselves. It's general consensus that those who play the role of celebrity are marionettes for faceless companies with vested interests in sucking the souls from unsuspecting commoners everywhere. Ergo, it's not sophisticated to enjoy what music plays on the radio. In order to maintain an air of decorum participants of the 21st century must do all that they can to remain individual and unique, but not too individual as to disrupt the status quo.

Echo explored her experiences with music growing up, how her favourite music never fit in with Narcissus' nor Felix's, both with so-called refined taste. How she worked hard to assimilate, to find music that was equal parts unheard of but widely appreciated. It was music taste that so often decided social cliques at school, and while Echo never did fit in, she prided herself on not being like the others. The others who would ridicule and torment her. She needed to be different to them, she needed to not want to fit in and be like them; that's the only way it could hurt less. She had built her younger identity around the image of being strange, liking music that sung about death and wanting to die, sticking safety pins through her ears and drawing all over her converse. That was the only thing she could control, in a sense, that carefully crafted identity. She refused to be mainstream.

In an interview with IZE soon after debuting in 2013, BTS leader Namjoon spoke about the identity of BTS, saying that they had to find a compromise between being a hip-hop group and an idol group. Both Namjoon and Yoongi had come from the underground rap scene and faced ridicule from peers for being part of an idol group. Just like in the West, celebrities or Idols are met with heavy criticism for being mainstream, enjoyed by the masses and therefore somehow lowbrow. In the case of Namjoon and Yoongi, they were criticised for even daring to dream of such a level of fame. Even though they were not yet famous, they were already sellouts by mere association. This was the same prejudice that Echo had found inside herself, originating in her tortured childhood, which manifested as a distaste for anything deemed popular, irrespective of quality. All she saw, just like Namjoon and Yoongi's critics, was quantity. A quantity, even a just desire for quantity, that seemingly cancelled out talent, message, meaning and purpose. The critics and Echo had one thing in common, though perhaps for different reasons. They were deeply threatened by the power that a mainstream artist could hold which stood in defiance of their own carefully crafted identity. They felt uncomfortable with the questions it made them ask of themselves, questioning a lifetime of conditioning.

BTS created a sense of tension in Echo's life, a tension between her desire to be individual and a desire to be a part of a collective. Her mind said *capitalism* and her heart said *art*; perhaps, she hoped, both could be real at the same time. This tension was only compounded by how she saw her friends and colleagues react to pop-music; it stood in defiance of the struggling regional arts world she was a part of. She felt she couldn't tell anyone yet, she couldn't share her newfound love. She didn't have enough information. It was like she was searching for something more so that she could elevate herself to be a sharpshooter for Bangtan.

Echo wanted to talk to them, to ask them what they thought about her thoughts. What their journey with music has been, what their journey with their identities has been. She wanted to ask them all the questions she was asking herself so that she might find the right way forward. She knew they were hated, she knew they were relegated to realms of ugly female hysteria. Yet that only made their music all the better. Though she felt the distance between them was large, she enjoyed the space it gave her to live in active resistance of the status quo. She thought such an act of resistance could only be achieved by listening to punk bands, but if BTS had taught her anything so far, it was that she suddenly knew nothing at all.

Although the realm of K-pop can come across quite foreign, as it is from a non-Western country, therefore quite literally foreign for those in the West, there are many historical examples of musicians and groups that have had similar trajectories to BTS. How people consume music has changed drastically over the past century, which in turn has shaped the way in which music is perceived and remembered by the masses. Ask anyone in the West who the biggest musicians or bands have been from the 1950s until the 90s and the answers are more than likely going to be the same; Elvis Presley, The Beatles, The Rolling Stones, The Monkees or Queen.

Ask anyone in the West who the biggest musicians or bands

have been from the 90s until current day and the answers will be far different. Not only because there are more musicians, more bands and more music consumers in the world, but because the way in which music is consumed has changed; we have seen a drastic decentralisation of power. Now with the decline of CD and digital sales, and the rise of music streaming, anyone can find success as a musician with the help of platforms like YouTube, or in the case of Lil Nas X, TikTok.

If we are to look at examples of groups with international influence, who set and break records and send crowds of young women into 'hysterics' then the field narrows considerably. In fact, it narrows to just two.

The first of which is The Beatles, who to this day are still considered to be the biggest band of all time. When looking at unit sales per music artist, they still very much are on top with 178 million units sold. When the British band rose to fame in the 1960s the term *Beatlemania* was used to describe the frenzied fans who would show up to concerts in support of their beloved band. These frenzied fans were largely female and were termed to be hysterical and referred to as *teenyboppers*; another way to dismiss the excitement and adoration of young women to the realms of immature adolescence. Yet it was these fans who drove the success of The Beatles. When their performance on The Ed Sullivan Show in 1964 was televised an estimated 73 million people tuned in. A considerable feat, considering, at the time, 73 million people was 22% of the global population; only 52 million households had televisions in the U.S. at the start of 1960. According to David Simonelli, The Beatles gave the opportunity for young women to show their spending power, and the ability to publicly express their sexual desires. This was an act of rebellion against a conservative society; a display of the sheer force of an untamed woman, something which continues to be exploited by mass-media to this day.

Fast forward to 2010 and another British act was set to take the world by storm, this time in the form of a boy band: One

Direction. Similar to the cultural technology process of creating an idol group, members from One Direction were solo auditionees for a popular talent show, X-Factor. Perhaps judge Simon Cowell had a copy of Lee's handbook on his bedside table for casual nighttime reading, for he gathered five young men who were not making it through to the next round and placed them into a group. They went on to come third on the talent show, much to the dismay of a rapidly building global fanbase. However, it didn't end there; after signing to Cowell's label, Syco, One Direction released an album in 2011 and went on to achieve global fame. Nearly 200 awards and 50 million record sales to date, One Direction went on hiatus in 2016 but are still regarded as a group akin to The Beatles. This isn't to say that The Beatles and One Direction have similar music, styles or interests. Rather, there is one thing that ties their journeys inextricably together: their fan base. The high-pitched screaming and deemed 'crazy' young girls at One Direction concerts left commentators and presenters throwing around the old *Beatlemania* term once again.

Both these musical acts, in the eyes of their fans and society more broadly, transcended from being *just* musicians to something more god-like; they were, and remain, idols, just like how an idol's ability to be an idol in South Korea is contingent on acquiring a devoted fan base. In many ways, from The Beatles to One Direction, an idol group is a reflection of the fans who support their every move. Fostering fans that not only unconditionally love their idols, like Christians love Jesus, but fans who show this outpouring of love with money—streaming and YouTube views, like sales of the Bible and door knocking to share *his good word*—is the number one priority of any group, musician or celebrity wanting to make it big. No wonder John Lennon said The Beatles were more popular than Jesus. It's the level of familiarity and loyalty fostered in religious groups that is also required of fans to make a group as big as The Beatles and One Direction. But it is argued that no one does it quite like

Idol

BTS. And perhaps they never will.

The continued success of BTS is attributed to their down-to-Earth nature; they remain seemingly genuine and humble through adversities and triumphs. Being humble is not often a character trait one would pair with an idol who must, to some degree, summon a carefully crafted mask to the surface in order to interact with fans on a global scale. Yet, by all means, it seems that BTS has retained much of what they began with; humility and humanity.

An idol walks no easy path, having to negotiate between what society asks of them; what their fans ask of them; what their company asks of them; what their loved ones ask of them; and what their heart truly desires. They could strike it lucky and the path could be something of a balance between varying competing interests, but circumstances like that are presumably few and far between.

Take Namjoon, for example, who struggled with balancing his raw rap style with K-pop elements which he discussed in an early vlog pre-debut from 2013. 방시혁, Bang Sihyuk, founder and co-CEO of Big Hit Entertainment, discovered Namjoon when he was 15 after listening to a mixtape of his, being told that this was what all the young people were listening to. So on the merit of his own talent, and after auditioning, Namjoon became the first member of BTS. Yet three years later he was still working on how to hone his skills and channel them into this new direction that was laid out before him.

What Namjoon wanted, presumably, was to do a good job so that BTS could debut, no doubt feeling this the most as the leader of the group. What Bang presumably wanted was for Namjoon to produce music that was commercially viable while staying true to its hip-hop origins. What society wanted was for BTS to fit into an easily labelled box of the stereotypical idol, and stay there. A box which, for many years, was one fans of K-pop deemed BTS not fit for in the first place. Namjoon was faced with feedback from his friends that his rapping wasn't as raw as it used to be; he wasn't as raw as he used to be.

Presumably, through the process of training to be an idol in an idol group who Namjoon was had changed, maybe not deep inside, but on the surface most definitely. He had no other choice but to assume many roles, the most important of which was the leader of BTS. A leader who had to represent a group that hadn't yet debuted and remain calm in the face of what was to come... an unknown future with many possibilities. But if he didn't do a good enough job BTS would not be able to debut, Namjoon and the rest of the group had to live in a state of flux. Working towards a future which could not be known, yet they had to operate under the assumption that something, anything, could happen and strive towards their goals despite never truly possessing the future to which they worked towards.

Here we can begin to see that in the early days Namjoon was balancing many interests, through this process he became Rap Monster, later, RM; his stage persona. But being an idol extends further beyond the stage; being an idol is a way of life. So in that sense, where does the idol stop and the human begin? When is Namjoon, Namjoon and RM, RM? Even within this chapter, it is hard to know which name to use, sometimes in YouTube videos it's Namjoon speaking, sometimes it's RM. Even when BTS speak to one another they move between stage and personal names; the lines are blurred, but maybe they have to be.

An idol is mass-made, shaped by social and cultural forces both locally and globally. An idol is a reflection of their country, their people and their fans. An idol is all the good in society, affluent; talented; humble; kind; intelligent; powerful; and beautiful. An idol is someone for the masses to model their lives upon. But it is not a society who shapes the truly admirable qualities of an idol, those qualities come from within. Dedication, loyalty, humility, self-reflexivity, and love.

These things are self-made, self-determined. The very fact that these are genuine character traits makes an idol all the better. No

Idol

company can force someone to be humble, it comes from within. What makes idols so great is that they're inherently human, they laugh and cry just like the rest of us. They're a beacon of hope to many striving for success in their own lives, living proof that anything is possible. A lot of pressure for a mere human, to have all eyes on them, to have every move scrutinised. Where human fails, persona prevails; but that's a story for Chapter Four.

When Echo drove down the highway towards the city for work she would listen to BTS' earlier songs and wonder what their lives would have been like then. She would superimpose herself into situations with them both in the past and present, each song holding a new idea for her to imagine and play with. Each time one of their songs came on shuffle she could feel her heart beat faster with excitement. Each time she watched a music video while she ate breakfast or lunch she would feel a sense of euphoria as she lived vicariously through them; singing and dancing for all to see.

She not only wanted to ask them questions to satiate her curiosity about them, but herself, as she sought to measure who she was by using sonar location in their general direction. It was a feeling she couldn't quite shake, the feeling that she already knew them so well and wanted them to know her, to love her, too. Sometimes she'd feel a pang in her heart when listening to a song, feeling the tension between her reality now and where she'd rather be, all too much to handle.

She would often let her mind wander and wonder, just so she could see what spending time with them would be like. She would cast each member in a scene, she would cook with Yoongi; she would dance with Hoseok; she would make up jokes with Seokjin; she would say morbid things to Taehyung; she would make films with Jungkook; she would play games with Jimin, and; she would go on long bike rides with Namjoon, shouting all her book recommendations at him over her shoulder.

She wondered if she could build a bridge with her words that would take her to them. She didn't know how, but she knew she had to meet them. Perhaps that was the thought that made their music even more exciting. They were her age, though they were idols they were familiar, which made her think they'd like her, too. There was a very real possibility that they could be friends. That's the promise that their music held; a future of excitement and euphoria with them. Each lyric, each beat, each move a piece to the puzzle that would show Echo the next step forward.

Though, as previously touched on, an idol is hated, they are loved on a scale most never see, nor truly experience for themselves. It is the idol's fans who provide a constant stream of love and affection, in the face of adversity and in moments of triumph. A fan is never far away from their idol, in spirit, at least. It is the existence of fans that characterises an idol group. When fans form together they become a powerful entity unto themselves; if the idol is to succeed, the bigger the entity, the better.

If it is the size of a fan group that sets apart idols and mere mortals, surely establishing and maintaining a fan group is of the utmost importance to anyone and everyone involved with K-pop. While the short story is, yes. The long story is, it's complicated.

You see, most people would consider themselves a fan of something or someone. But to what degree? Do most people go to see their favourite musician in concert? Sure. Do most people watch music videos of their favourite band online? Of course. Do most people pool their money to take out billboard ad space in Times Square to promote their idols? Well... do you? Perhaps what we're seeing now more than ever is the rise of the superfan; someone who goes above and beyond for their beloved idol. Someone who stays up all night streaming tracks to help their favourite group get to number one, someone who undertakes fan projects to raise money for a charity on behalf of their idol, someone who lives and breathes their beloved. As mentioned before, it's a religious-level feat needed to take a large number

Idol

of people from normal members of society to super-fan to rival the likes of BTS' fan group, ARMY. If the question is how does an idol group, like BTS, get fans as powerful as ARMY? The answer then surely must be parasocial kin.

According to doctoral students Nomi-Kaie Bennett, Amy Rossmeisl, Karisma Turner, Billy Holcombe, Robin Young, Tiffany Brown and Heather Key, parasocial refers to a one-sided relationship. In this one-sided relationship there is a person, in this context the fan, who spends a lot of energy and time in the consumption of content and interaction from the celebrity, or idol, who is unaware of the other's existence. Of interesting note is the use of the term *persona* instead of celebrity or idol in the original article from the authors. Which is to say that it is not the true identity of a celebrity or idol that the fan is interested in, rather something more socially constructed. A persona perhaps socially constructed for the express purpose of such consumption, but more on that in Chapter Four.

In 2012, six months before their debut, BTS started to post videos to YouTube which gave their small audience a chance to feel like they knew the to-be idols personally. These videos created the illusion of a face-to-face relationship, inviting the audience to become a lifelong friend. The content which BTS released matured and grew over time, along with the group and their fan base who were treated to behind the scenes glimpses into the idol's lives each week through their channel *BangtanTV*. Complementary to this was BTS' ability to interact directly with their fans through Twitter and fancafes, proving to the fans that these connections weren't just make-believe; there was actually a BTS member reaching out and talking to them. Through this, fans familiarity with BTS grew, as did their parasocial bond. Bang said in an interview with Time that it was loyalty built through direct contact with fans that led to the U.S. success of BTS.

Originally, parasocial kin was the term used as it was intended that fans feel like family members, this is seen in the writing of Joanna Elfving-Hwan. Which, of course, some of them do;

65

even more so now that ARMY is self-directed and claims to be a family unto itself. However, is it really a family connection that fans want, or that BTS is selling to their audience? Perhaps it is something more; for what is a fan to do with a lyric coming from BTS asking to be tied up so they can't run away?

Bennett et al. write that parasocial relationships closely align to in-real-life connections. They are voluntary, provide companionship and are influenced by social attraction. The feelings of gratitude, affection, longing, encouragement and loyalty not only are expressed from the fan to an idol but from an idol to a fan. In many ways the feelings within the parasocial relationship, to a certain degree, are mutual. However, the power dynamic is what remains unchecked. The largest difference of all, is that the idol needn't know the fans' name. For BTS, the fans' name is ARMY.

A week later Echo found herself carried to different music videos by the algorithm, ones she hadn't seen before. Her heart raced once again as she was thrust into another set, another world to explore with BTS by her side. It was as if she could walk into the music video and stand before each member as they danced, she could look at the art that hung on the walls and hear her shoes squeak on the marble floors. Today, it was the music video for *Blood Sweat & Tears* that she came across for the first time, stumbling into the brightly lit museum while BTS breezed past. Their outfits were renaissance inspired; loud prints and smooth hair. The museum featured renaissance art such as The Fall of the Rebel Angels by Pieter Bruegel with references to the folklore of Icarus, which, Echo noticed, tied into other themes shown in earlier music videos. They give a glimpse of what is referred to as the *BTS Universe*, an alternate timeline of sorts. Echo found the *Blood Sweat & Tears* clip to be quite extravagant, elegant and eloquent; it showed BTS as more than just young men. For the first time, Echo was seeing BTS not only as objects of sexual desire, but young men expressing their own temptations through dance, lingering suggestive eye contact and lyrics such as "tie me up so I can't run away, grab me tight and shake me up so I can't come to my senses".

Up until this point she had been viewing BTS as brothers, of sorts, close friends who she had been getting to know over time. But now, watching them through a more sexualised lens, she was, just by watching, perpetuating their newfound status as an object in her mind. She didn't like that. She felt like she was intruding on their privacy by watching them dance that way. And yet, she was entranced and couldn't tear her eyes from the screen. She felt like she was breaking a rule; she pushed many thoughts away and told herself this was for research, not consumption. In her mind, she started to add new dimensions to the idols, ones she knew were already there. Now it was as if they had given her permission to study them both as subject and object, which only created further tension between Echo's conflicting ideals.

This tension propelled her to new areas of thought, it brought an element of adventure back into her life. Most of all, it made her want to write again, something she hadn't felt compelled to do for many years, yet desired so innately that she dreamed of her pen gliding over paper as much as she dreamt of BTS themselves.

Another characteristic of an idol, similar to being simultaneously mass and self-made, is that they must operate as both object and subject. Idols are intentionally manufactured, a term not often used in relation to a human subject. Idols are an object which is shaped from human to persona. Idols often operate under a top-down management system but also have autonomy, to the same degree that anyone does, over their own lives. For an idol to be successful they must be a malleable object that is shaped by an entertainment company in accordance with tried-and-true methods. They must submit themselves to objectification from fans, society and the media, as this is how

Idol Limerence

they are sold to the masses. An idol must be an active agent in the co-creation of their idol image and the maintenance of their public and personal selves; as such, they need to be a subject at the same time.

More often than not an idol can be deemed inhuman, devoid of emotion, or as previously suggested, a marionette of sorts. Fans talk about idols on public forums like pieces of meat, fans love them so much they could, in their own words, eat the idol whole. Even in direct conversation with idols, such as when they're streaming a live video and able to see all comments on a screen before them, fans continue to objectify their beloved. Why? Because an idol is an object designed specifically for mass-consumption; the desire of the idol as an object manifests in a variety of ways, including their perpetual sexualisation. More on that in Chapter Six.

However, at the same time as being an object, a subject, an idol is human. As previously discussed, it is those human qualities that make an idol irresistible. An idol is unattainable with their wealth and affluence, seemingly hundreds of levels above us commoners who slog our guts out doing the tedious 9-5. But also, an idol remains attainable with their overt heterosexuality and lack of a visible romantic partner. An idol surely must have to come to terms with their status as a sexual and emotional object, find a way to justify it to themselves, their friends and family. An idol then surely must play an active role in the maintenance of their perpetual objectification. An idol is their own object and subject, an idol, in many ways, is a complex contradiction. Just like the tension Echo experiences between her competing interests and selves creating better thoughts, more inspiration, the same goes for an idol; their complexity is how they thrive.

Though an idol is mass-and-self-made, object and subject, they are not without power. In fact, it is these very elements that position the idol in such a way that they can transcend cultural, social and physical boundaries; an idol is powerful. Who else but an idol has a following in the millions from countries across the globe? No political figure has such sway, the only other comparable entity is a religion. So if an idol is a modern religious figure for the masses, what is to stop them from changing the world? Spoiler: not a whole lot. But that's a story for Chapters Seven and Eight. The point is: an idol can have huge social, cultural and economic power.

Further, it is no mistake that the top groups, musicians, performers, K-pop or otherwise, are men. If an idol is a reflection of society, then an idol is the smiling face of patriarchy and capitalism. No one benefits from systemic inequalities in the same way an idol does, though not quite the same as a mining magnate or a warlord; a male idol perpetuates gender norms and asserts themselves as a dominant force within the music industry.

An idol has more power than the fan who got them to where they are. No matter how much an idol may love their fans the inequalities remain. An idol can only be an idol within a capitalist society; an idol can only exist at the expense of their fans. One is powerful and the other, less so. One makes a profit from the other and rarely is it the other way around. It only remains ethical for as long as the fan willingly participates, but that in itself is up for debate.

Lastly comes the most important element of all in the study of the complex phenomenon of idol: an idol is powerless and human. Though they are indeed powerful and the well-groomed face of capitalism, their very ability to be as such is contingent on their vulnerabilities. No, they're not robots or aliens. They're imperfect, living, breathing humanoids, or at least the assumption is that they are, in this chapter anyway. If this assumption is correct then this final complexity makes idols the perfect contradiction; powerful and powerless at the same time. Though it must be noted that a powerless idol is still ten times more powerful than the author of this book, they remain powerless all the same; a comforting thought for the masses. This contradiction leads to friction which is where all the good things happen; as it was said before, where human fails persona prevails... and you can't have one without the other.

In a video recorded for BTS' sixth birthday celebration, otherwise known as a Festa, in 2018, Yoongi discusses his concerns about what would happen if he were to lose everything.

'I'm afraid of falling, but not landing,' he says.

Jimin notes he had been wondering what he was living for earlier in the year.

An idol is not immune to failure, in fact an idol must work twice as hard to maintain their position or risk losing it all. After five years as a group, and many more spent training, who would the individual members be if BTS were to no longer exist? Though an idol is active in the maintenance of their success it is not always up to them if they continue on or not; they could get dropped by their company, they could say or do the wrong thing and be shunned, they could fall ill and not be able to perform.

A topical example is the fact that South Korea has mandatory military service for male citizens which lasts 18-22 months; BTS are no exception to this rule. Or rather, if they are to conscientiously object they will be shunned by their country. To not serve is to disrespect the nation. However, in order to serve they must put their lives and careers on hold for nearly two years. That's a long time in the entertainment industry. How BTS and Big Hit navigate military enlistment at the height of the group's fame remains to be seen, it is reported that the eldest, Seokjin, may have to enlist by the end of 2020.

As demonstrated by Yoongi and Jimin in the 2018 birthday celebration video, an idol's mental health can be heavily impacted upon by their own success and their perceived ability to lose it all in the blink of an eye. Their lives consist of long days and longer nights spent rehearsing, in interviews, writing, recording, travelling and performing. This means that irrespective of how an idol may feel mentally or physically, the show must go on.

Only once a musician takes on the idol persona does a fan take interest. If K-pop is an ocean and an idol must sink or swim, where exactly does the audience's interest lie? A human must exist outside of the water, but an idol must voluntarily drown themselves in order to maintain their position, metaphorically at least. So if it's sink or swim for BTS, which will they choose? They must balance both, a delicate act of dying on the global stage for their ARMY, a subtle act of swimming in their personal time for their sanity. As this chapter's subtitle suggests, though it is the human side to idols that the fans like, it is only the idol persona that creates the fan in the first place. Only above the surface of the water do they, the idol, breathe, and the interest in them ends.

An idol is loved and hated; mass and self-made; fan focussed, fan-driven and a reflection of the fans as a whole. An idol is also an object and subject; artist and muse, and; a culmination of culture and history. Lastly, an idol is powerful and capitalistic, and powerless and human. History has not shown anyone who has exemplified the complex and dualistic nature of idol, celebrity, musician, artist, nor muse, quite like BTS. Instead of giving an overview of BTS' achievements, the elements of what comprises their idol role were briefly examined. This was done intentionally, it is not the aim of this chapter, nor book, to try and capture all of BTS' history from underdog to new heights of fame unseen before; that is deserving of a book unto itself. Rather, the aim of this chapter was to begin to illustrate the complexity of an industry, K-pop, which creates idols and is the context of a group that is, according to this book at least, a profound cultural phenomenon. A phenomenon that creates more phenomena in its image.

This concept will be expanded upon in coming chapters through a deep-dive on the driving force behind BTS: love. It is important to note here that this is merely an introductory text on the phenomenon of love, limerence and how it intersects with, builds and shapes other cultural phenomena. For some, this book will be the first insight into who BTS are, too. There will be many intentional gaps to come so that we may continue to grow and add to our knowledge together in the future.

Further, it is important to construct and show BTS as human beings who had humble beginnings, and remain humble while continuing to reach heights no other group has before. Not only are they experiencing success in their home country of Korea, but also international success which is driven mostly by their ARMY. BTS to date still haven't received mainstream recognition in the West, having just experienced a royal snub from the Grammys in late 2019 with no nomination. However, this has not managed to slow their pace, nor their accolades, nor their swelling fan base which grows every minute. What BTS shows the West is that the days of centralised industry power are over. They don't need a Grammy to sell out stadiums or contribute nearly $5 billion U.S. to the Korean economy each year, as reported by the Hyundai Research Institute, nor does any other musician.

In the face of discrimination and prejudice BTS has risen time and time again, in their wake an ARMY follows them willingly into the darkness. An ARMY determined to show the world that what matters to them, BTS, should be legitimised in the eyes of as many people and cultural institutions as possible. This begins to show a fascinating symbiosis which will be further examined later in this book; neither BTS nor ARMY can exist without the other. But perhaps the question is: can either live while the other survives? If love is indeed a flower, like the one Echo watched wither away or the one that blooms in a number of BTS music videos, then what does that mean for ARMY who loves BTS, and BTS who loves them back?

It was March and Echo had a new way of being in the world. Each step was lighter than the one before and she seemingly floated through the monotony of her day, propelled forward by the songs that made up the soundtrack to her life. She curated playlists to conjure different moods at different times, she changed between one for power and another for inspiration throughout the day depending on the task at hand. In her mind she walked along the river with the members, laughing and playing. In her reality she was staring up at the trees and writing prose; seemingly a page a minute, as if she were receiving downloads from the universe to the beat of a love song. She wanted to be stronger, faster, better at everything, she wanted to be born anew each and every day, better than the day before. Suddenly, everything had to have more meaning, it was like the volume had turned up on her life, along with it the brightness; she felt everything tenfold. Half way through March she fronted to her gym and signed up for a powerlifting competition, which was to take place in August.

"Are you sure?" her trainer asked her, "it's not going to be easy."

Echo nodded slowly.

"I want to compete in the Under 57 class," she added.

His eyebrows rose.

"You could compete in Under 63 without cutting weight," he suggested.

Echo shrugged.

"I want a challenge."

"I don't want to break you."

She smiled.

"You won't."

Instead of Tchaikovsky, it was BTS that rang in Echo's ears as she began to train for competition. Instead of dancing, auditioning, she loaded her spine, her hips, her shoulders, until she broke through to a new reality of consciousness. She pushed so far past her own limitations that she began to breathe in a new mentality. This was the only way she could perform under pressure or perform to a crowd. The process gave her new avenues to dream, but the true euphoria came from the stillness of her mind when she unracked a weight that scared her to death. In a sense it

Idol Limerence

was a kind of death, just her and the bar; not a thought in sight. While BTS surrounded her, serenaded her, she ceased to exist for a fraction of a second as she descended into a squat. Time under tension, under pressure; this was how her star would be born.

Persona

Have I lost myself or have I gained you?
—Singularity, BTS

'Can you hear me? I don't want this anymore. I want to call it off,' shouts Joel as he kneels on a frozen lake in the dead of night.

Joel has erased painful memories of Clementine, an ex-girlfriend. In the process of this, he has managed to excruciatingly relive each failed moment of their relationship. More importantly, he has relived the tender ones which had become repressed during the messy breakup. Each scene he relives eventually becomes blurry and fades away. Joel becomes self-aware within his memories and actively tries to change scenes, moments, in the past. He convinces Clementine to run and hide with him so that they can remain together in his mind. As Clementine had also undergone memory erasure in real life, inside his mind was the only place they could exist together now, and he was desperate to hold onto her. Inevitably, Clementine is forcefully dragged away from Joel, scene after scene. Eventually, he forgets her entirely.

When Echo watched *Eternal Sunshine of the Spotless Mind* at age eleven, she took it as pure fact for one key reason; the movie showed her, larger than life, exactly what the inside of her head looked like. She was Clementine and Joel was Narcissus. Later on, Joel would become Felix. The scene on the ice would be Echo in her mind garden, begging for the limerence to stop, that was, until BTS showed up and erased Felix from existence, along with every heartbreak that came before him. Like the weight from the barbell that Echo loved for numbing her never-resting mind, BTS pressed down on every corner of her consciousness until the sadness had no more space to exist; only they prevailed.

If Goffman is correct when he says that we form our identity through every day interactions with others, then it was at this point that Echo's identity began to shift on its axis. No longer was she having a simple *everyday* interaction with another person, she was having an abnormal interaction with a group of idols in her mind. That being said, it most definitely became an everyday occurrence.

Upon waking each morning Echo would find herself already mid-way through an interaction with BTS in her mind.

"What makes you say that?" Yoongi asks.

"I don't know," Echo replies, "just a feeling."

A feeling about what? Echo wonders as she swings her legs out of bed.

The conversation became inaudible while Echo moved about her room and prepared for the day. After breakfast she had forgotten about the conversation entirely, reality had set in and she was late for a meeting.

In these conversations that came in and out of Echo's consciousness, she reflected on herself through menial conversation. Often times these conversations would be short-lived, just one or two exchanges in an empty room. A rehearsal room one day, a dressing room the next. Why she was in these rooms with BTS was an unsolved mystery; did she work with them? Did they invite her there? Are they friends?

Echo soon became self-aware in these interactions, realising that she could continue on these dreams after waking in an imaginary state. Usually inside these imagined scenarios, she was more of an energy, an entity, just a mass with no features that she knew to be Echo. After the second week of waking up to conversations in full flight, however, Echo began to insert herself more actively into the story as she went about her day. Originally she had thought of specific interactions that revolved around first meeting BTS from an objective standpoint, curious as to how they would react to her. Now, her imagination sprawled out before her as her consciousness expanded to new depths to better accommodate her so-called social experiments.

Goffman writes that in our everyday interactions we are actors with a predetermined role, however, that doesn't mean that we can't pick and choose our lines. We make up our identity through the retelling of stories of events, ideas, places and times that have shaped us. They needn't be entirely true, but they do need to come across as genuine and believable. In that sense, each of our identities can be understood as more of a mask. Something we co-create with external social, economic, environmental and political factors, to act as our public-facing selves.

Through these imagined interactions in her mind, Echo began to create a new role for herself. Though she was still very much Echo-the-nearly-26-year-old-wanna-be-writer, she found new ways of framing herself that were more desirable to the made-up meetings with BTS. The new Echo fit the narrative better; she had nice hair and nice clothes and nice skin. Everything she wished she could have and more. To go with these new aesthetics Echo began to craft a back story to explain how she got to being in these ever-changing rooms with the most famous group on the planet. In her dreams she moonlighted as a reporter, a lawyer, a designer, a painter, a model, a stylist. It was suddenly a *Choose Your Own Adventure: BTS Edition* and Echo was Player 1. Each time her daily BTS YouTube playlist began to play while she got ready for work, her mind would wander through the limitless possibilities.

Through the use of our imaginations, said to be unique to us as humans, we are able to see and talk about things that don't exist. We could change the colour of our hair, nip and tuck at our body until it were more desirable, dress in the most lavish outfits and have more charming character traits. We could give ourselves friends who care for us, family that is functional and all the riches in the world.

Mead writes that through the use of our imagination we are able to put ourselves in the shoes of others and see ourselves through their eyes. We balance this view of ourselves with the image of how we want ourselves to be perceived, and who we really wish to be. We communicate these desires, these imagined perspectives and traits, through language and symbols. These can be quite literal symbols, like tattoos or odd-shaped earrings, but these can also be things that are symbolic of something else entirely. In chapter one it was a red dress, the same red dress that Echo wore in chapter two to convey her new 'I'm powerful and desirable and I don't give a damn' attitude. This message was conveyed not only through the colour of her dress, but the fact that she was wearing a dress at all. Echo knew how it would be perceived if she were to show up at a party where no one else was wearing a dress, where everyone else was a few levels shy of smart casual. When she chose the dress she knew how she'd be viewed; it would be close to scandalous. By wearing something out of place she was sending a message; she couldn't care less what anyone thought of her. She knew that The Pound would be full of drunken young men who would find that statement rather charming, alluring, daring. Ironic, seeing as she was aiming for 'fuck-all-men'; perhaps a different use of the word was subconsciously intended after all.

Neuroscientist David Eagleman says in the documentary, *The Creative Brain*, that when we use our imagination we are able to unhook our brains from the present place and time and travel elsewhere. Through this we are able to try new ideas, experiment with things that do not yet exist and bring them forth from the unknown to the known. This is an integral part to the creative process, we are inherently creative. Not limited to the realms of art, we are creators, creators of ideas, places, spaces, objects... creators of worlds. So if we are able to unhinge our minds from here and now to travel elsewhere in order to imagine and create: where exactly is it that we end up?

Echo had mastered the use of her imagination, originally, to create a sacred nighttime garden where she grew flowers and herbs and spent time nurturing her feelings for others. Now, it was a place to recreate herself in the eyes of her newly found idols. She imagined what they'd think of her, what they'd like and dislike about her appearance and her character. After a month of imagining the Echo she'd rather be, she started to take steps in reality towards becoming someone BTS would want to be around. Instead of being passive like she had been when she was in love with Felix, Echo now actively sought out the aspects of herself that she didn't like or wanted to shy away from. It was like there were seven huge floodlights on her named Namjoon, Seokjin, Yoongi, Hoseok, Jimin, Taehyung and Jungkook that illuminated every inch of her being. Through their eyes Echo was finally able to stand face-to-face with her body and all the trauma that she had been harbouring for the better part of 25 years.

It wasn't pretty. There were tantrums and tears as she began to analyse past mistakes and accept her wrongdoings. Throughout it all, she kept her eyes firmly on her goal: be someone BTS would want to be around, be Super Echo.

After being shamed out of her film degree during her first year of university, Echo had changed her major to sociology. Preferring to study the masses rather than write for them, she absorbed theory upon theory about the economy, social structures, religion, the environment and abnormal psychology. She used this knowledge to better understand the world around her, instead of writing for the screen she began to write personal essays about political conflicts, environmental harm and animal abuse. A welcomed change to the torturous romantic fables she was conditioned to writing. Sometimes she would use this knowledge to deconstruct herself, but only briefly, often placing Freudian-level problems in the too-hard basket. An avid fan of Marx, Echo was staunchly against capitalism and did all she could to not be consumerist; though she knew she had to be an active member of a capitalistic society in order to change it. Half way through her degree Echo realised she had to make amends with living as a contradiction, ethically being anti-capitalist while benefiting from consumerism with her iPhone and MacBook and the scores of books that lined her walls. Her money and status allowed her to freely acquire new knowledge, she could change in and out of subjects like it didn't cost a few thousand dollars each time. As much as she tried to avoid it, she was a capitalistic, privileged white person.

While Echo was constructing scenarios of BTS in her mind she was also deconstructing every aspect of the idol group. She counted the hours she spent poring over YouTube videos each day as sociological research. Maybe she would write a paper on how Korean men could still be masculine while wearing sparkly blouses and rapping; maybe she could explore performative aggressive masculinities by analysing BTS' old live performances and categorising them based on hip thrusts and feverish growls. None of that interested her the same way their identities did; Echo was transfixed by their ability to perform the role of idol and boy-next-door. They moved between the roles on stage and in interviews as easily as breathing. Echo felt such a level of familiarity with them that only drove this desire further; how could her peers be so similar to her, yet so different? How could they know exactly what she wanted to see and exactly what she wanted to hear, in songs, in interviews, in vlogs. Echo's spidey senses were tingling; a small voice suggested that perhaps she had fallen into a bigger capitalistic plot. But that's not what worried her the most. She was afraid that she didn't care about being a pawn in a consumerist game at all. Consequences of capitalism be damned; she wanted seven Korean husbands and she wanted them *now*.

The days passed and Echo's feelings for BTS grew, which she labelled as *it's complicated* and pushed to the side. If she thought with her head, she would say that she was duped into fantasising about the group day in and out, just like millions of other fans around the world. It was all too easy, it was as if she had fallen right into a well laid trap. All algorithms led back to BTS, just like all of Echo's thoughts. However, if she thought with her heart she would say that this was a predestined meeting of old friends; she was always meant to discover BTS, perhaps so her newly formed research could help change the world. *It's complicated*, indeed, especially when Echo refused to admit what was staring her right in the face all along.

Echo had so many questions for her idol group. She wanted to know how self-aware they were; did they know they were part of a capitalist plot to win the hearts and minds of young women all around the world? Are they aware that they have identities which they use for every aspect of idol life? Were they an active part of creating these identities? And most of all, Echo wanted to know how they felt trying to grow up in the public eye. She struggled day in and out trying to figure out who she was and there were no eyes on her, she wanted to know what it felt like to be a millennial with the weight of the world on their shoulders. For this exploration she turned her attention to leader Namjoon; something always brought Echo back to RM.

He was articulate; his English was good; he was thoughtful; he was self-aware, and most of all; Echo related to his words as if they were her own, many times she was convinced they were. When Echo first watched *Idol* it was RM who was first on the screen, she remembered how for a fraction of a second she thought she knew him from somewhere. A fleeting familiarity in the beginning, now a familiarity she shared with the whole idol group.

Echo conducted interview after interview with Namjoon in the room inside her head. She asked a thousand questions then asked the same ones again, but in different ways. Pretending she knew what he'd reply with based on her many hours of careful online research.

"Does your idea of who you are change?" Echo asks, sitting on the edge of a long couch opposite Namjoon.

"Yes," Namjoon replies, "it can be hard to know who I am when so many people are telling me who to be."

Echo nods, looking down at her hands.

"Who are you today?"

"I'm just me," he smiles, "that's all I know."

By March 28, Echo had watched every music video BTS released and heard every song they ever wrote. Slowly but surely she was forming an argument in her mind, a long form essay that she desperately needed to write. Not only was she sure she was made to become fascinated and besotted, but she was sure BTS themselves were active parts in the creation of their idol identities and the way that they were packaged and sold as love commodities. Echo had read messages on forums from young girls claiming they were madly in love with Jungkook, saying they couldn't breathe without him. Echo wondered what that felt like, Echo wondered if it were possible to fall in love with an idol despite the idol and the single-sided relationship being intentionally fabricated. Did that mean it wasn't love? Were these young people simply just obsessed, just delusional? Echo believed all the answers to lie within the mind of the idols themselves, if only she could find a way to get inside their brains and poke around; imagine all the things she could write if she knew what made them tick.

What Echo didn't know, however, was that she was about to be swept up in what is known as a *comeback*; BTS were preparing for the release of their newest album.

Persona

It was a Friday night and Echo, as always, was minding her own business when she was cosmically pulled towards her laptop and urged to refresh YouTube.

There was a new video from *ibighit*, Big Hit Entertainment's YouTube account, the first release from BTS' forthcoming album.

Echo couldn't believe her eyes.

When she saw the thumbnail her heart nearly jumped from her chest and onto the screen. Her eyesight blurred slightly.

Her breaths were short. Shallow.

Her hands shook as she rushed to click on the video.

It was RM, *just* RM.

And it wasn't only that, it was the name of the clip that made her stare in wonder.

There, right before her very eyes, was the music video for *Persona*.

All her birthdays had come at once.

"Be careful what you wish for," Echo said aloud to herself as she pressed play.

Analytical psychologist Carl Jung writes that a *persona* is a social face that an individual presents to the world, a mask of sorts. This is used for social integration and adaptation in a variety of situations; in the workplace; at a new school; in a new friendship group. This mask conceals the true face of the individual, the true self, which is inherently flawed. In some ways this mask could help to give the individual a sense of confidence, for it is not really them who they are showing to the world, and their true emotions are protected from harm. They cannot be rejected if it is not their true self who stands before a crowd in the first place. Further, a persona can help protect one's identity, and provide a separation between personal and public. Many influences impact a persona, as it operates as a means to better fit in, so presumably personas look different depending on elements such as class, geo-political locations, family structure, the environment and the individual's ego, unconscious and shadow self.

From a young age we are asked 'who are you?' and we are expected to answer with a pre-made sentence that adequately communicates the very core of our being. Our childhood, while we negotiate the often turbulent social landscape of primary school and beyond, is where the persona is initially formed. We construct our identity through everyday conversations and interactions, we use our imagination to see how others view us and adjust accordingly in order to fit in. Over time our persona builds through this process, the sum of an array of life experiences, internal and external forces. We use this as our do-it-yourself personality, something we can add to and subtract from, if we so please.

The music video for *Persona* opened on a white haired RM standing in a classroom, reminiscent of *Boy in Luv*. He stands in greeting as if he were the teacher, or spiritual leader about to deliver a sermon. Quite literally saying 'yo' while looking up at the camera, head tilted to the side, channeling a blend of mischievous bad-boy and quiet scholar in street clothes.

Just like when Echo watched *Idol* for the first time, she was transported.

She didn't know where she went during her first BTS multi-dimensional trip, but this time she knew exactly where and when she was.

It was like all her weeks of research and mind-body-soul devotion to exploring the BTS universe had prepared her for this comeback.

The very existence of such a song, such a video clip made Echo think that perhaps this was legilimency; where she was provided such a clandestine look into the thoughts and feelings of BTS. Their music, their craft was perhaps witchcraft instead... idolcraft, if you may.

For just like in Harry Potter, legilimency can go both ways,

Persona

and Echo now felt like, somehow, Namjoon had sensed her poking around in his persona, his secret mind garden, and created this song, this moment in time for her eyes, and ears, alone.

With each thundering beat of her heart Echo travelled through time and space in the direction of RM. As if the classroom where he stood grew larger, and larger, and larger, until its walls stretched out from the screen and hurtled past Echo's head.

Their eyes met across the internet.

He blinked.

She blinked.

When Echo opened her eyes again she was standing face to face with RM, not Namjoon. He was standing so close she thought she was going to fall into his eyes. Though the headphones in her ears tied her physical body to the present, she couldn't feel a vessel anymore. It was like she was bodiless, or rather she was the embodiment of something else entirely.

He was different to what she had imagined Namjoon to be, though there was a glimmer of him she could faintly see when she quickly turned her head to look around the room. It was like RM was an optical illusion, if she wanted to see Namjoon she couldn't look RM in the eye; she had to look just over his shoulder for him to appear.

Though she was certain he was 5'9" and she was 5'5" they stood eye to eye.

His energy towered over her and pressed down, it was electric. Urgent.

He wanted to talk, but they didn't have to exchange words.

RM drew Echo's attention back to the lyrics as the song played from the beginning, on repeat. Suddenly, Echo could understand Korean and the song took on a new meaning.

RM smiled and nodded, this is why he brought her here, to this moment.

'*Who am I' the question I had my whole life.*

Echo looked at RM, eyes wide, confused.

"Do you want me to help you figure it out?" she asked.

RM shook his head and extended a long finger towards Echo. Echo looked down to where his finger pointed.

"Me?" she said softly.

RM nodded. He wanted Echo to do that thing again, that thing where she related all of BTS' lyrics back to herself.

His eyes were smiling, all knowing.

Echo suddenly got the impression that he knew every place her mind had been, as if every time she thought about him he was alerted to an intruder stepping on his well toiled soil. Instead of apprehending her he had chosen to fall back and observe. In this garden, just like her own, time wasn't linear and barely existed at all. Echo realised she must have been there for millennia. Echo realised he had been watching her the whole time, waiting for this moment of reciprocity where they could stand face to face.

Echo tried not to be shy, reminding herself that she was almost 26 and could absolutely pretend to have her shit together in front of a make-believe vision of Kim Namjoon's constructed persona. She was just glad she never googled past girlfriends or shirtless pictures, now that would be something to get embarrassed over.

RM replayed the song from the start, urging Echo to pay attention.

"Who am I?" Echo asked aloud.

RM nodded his head slowly, eyebrows raised, waiting for a response.

The walls of the room began to move again as they were both transported back in time. Memories whirled about them, snapshots that ran into one another. RM watched each of them come and go with a sense of quiet familiarity; Echo wondered if he had been here before.

There was Narcissus, smiling and laughing as he and Echo rolled down a hill when they were seven.

Echo and RM crouched behind a structure atop the Elephant House at the Moulin Rouge, watching Christian sing to Satine.

Persona

They disappeared down the stairs towards Satine's bedroom.

RM walked out into the open and Echo followed. He tapped his foot as they stared out at a Paris they had never seen before.

He was keeping time to something that Echo couldn't hear or feel or see.

RM nodded his head and turned to Echo.

"Are you ready?" he smiled.

Echo looked at him with wide eyes, these were his first words to her.

He winked.

Fireworks erupted from the Elephant House.

Brilliant orbs of light floated down from on high around them both. They stood there for a moment, once again eye to eye, a thousand unsaid words between them.

The world shifted, and they began to travel through Echo's earliest memories once again.

Echo carving Narcissus' name into the table, Narcissus telling Echo he liked someone else, Echo crying in her bedroom, in her bathroom, on her way to school, on her way home from school.

This is making me uncomfortable, Echo thought.

RM shot her a look, reminding her he could probably hear everything inside her head, as it was inside her head where they currently stood.

Echo stood still and watched her life flash before her eyes.

Reliving each moment that built her persona, analysing each interaction over and over.

It wasn't just memories played out like movie scenes that they saw. It was thoughts and feelings somehow projected in colour and vibration throughout a tiny white room where they suddenly stood.

Echo saw so many sides to herself that she was ashamed of, she remembered all the things that she pushed beneath the surface of her conciousness. Traits that she thought wouldn't be desirable, thoughts she knew no one would understand.

She shook her head and turned away, hoping if her eyes were

shut RM wouldn't be able to see what she could see. She had a darker side, one she hadn't faced in years, one she didn't want to face while he was present.

Echo's eyes opened again and RM was back facing her, eerily close.

He shook his head, once again directing her attention to the lyrics.

My shadow, I wrote and called it 'hesitation'.

"Your shadow?" Echo mused.

She thought about RM's shadow self, Namjoon's shadow self; just like her, he had a dark side too. Not luxuriously dark, not the kind of darkness that Echo would wear like a badge of honour when she was dressed all in black with safety pins for earrings. Just gross, ugly, undesirable things that don't fit with the persona, that are strange and awkward and make people uncomfortable.

Echo's heart fluttered, but not the good flutter like she got at the start of the music video. Perhaps more of a stutter, a falter, she knew she was flawed but she was too scared to look. A spiral was inevitable, she was afraid she would fall if she were to examine her shadow self up close, to give it words and an output. She was afraid it would demonstrate to her and ever-watching RM that she wasn't worthy of her own hopes and dreams.

RM feverishly shook his head as the room grew larger.

They were back in the classroom of the music video, sitting off to the side as they watched RM perform to the camera.

"Are you paying attention?" RM whispered.

He spoke again, Echo thought.

Yes, RM blinked, *now watch the other me.*

The flaws of mine that I know, maybe that's all I've got really.

The room moved again, faster this time. More recent memories swirled around Echo and RM while her mind churned over each moment where her shadow self surfaced or was pushed beneath. There were so many interactions that Echo couldn't focus, there was an older Narcissus, the five-minute boyfriends that came after him, the friendships that came as rapidly as they went, then Felix. Their relationship played out in the blink of an eye, each moment spent together was condensed into a nanosecond and played in succession.

Then, they were free falling, RM and Echo, through the air as darkness swallowed them both.

What's going on? Echo tried to find RM in the darkness.

I don't know, this is your head, not mine, he replied.

A small crack of light appeared in the distance, illuminating Echo and RM who stood shoulder to shoulder, watching as it grew closer.

With it came a wave of noise, louder and louder.

Echo looked at RM, scared.

RM smiled, as if he knew what was coming.

This is going to be good, he ran at the brightness as it hurtled towards them.

Echo froze and watched as it washed over her.

Her head spun with the technicolour churn of excitement and celebration that surrounded them. Rainbow confetti fell from the sky and a giant dragon circled around them. They stood in the middle of the *Idol* music video. BTS danced next to them, faces swimming in and out of view.

"Oh," Echo looked around, "oh, no..."

"What's this all about, Echo?" RM stood in front of her again. Smiling. Omnipotent.

He knew what it was all about, he just wanted to see if she'd say it.

The room changed again as they were thrown through a retrospective of Echo discovering the BTS universe. Every mouse click, every picture viewed, every note taken was displayed before them. RM moved the memories throughout the air with his hands, reading what Echo thought with great interest.

Nope, Echo thought, *this is too much.*

RM whipped around, opening his mouth to say something but it was too late.

Echo changed the scene, bringing them back to the music video where RM stood in the classroom.

"I'm ready for the next part," Echo looked at RM out the corner of her eye, "I'm paying attention," she added.

RM sighed, turning to watch himself.

My name is R.
The 'me' that I remember and people know.
The 'me' that I created myself to vent out.

Echo looked at RM.

"Are you going to make the room move again?"

RM shrugged.

"Let me guess," Echo sighed, "it was me making the room move all along."

RM gave a smug smile.

"Ok, ok," Echo moved her hands around like she saw RM doing before.

The room changed back to plain white.

Three other Echos stood before them, there was Echo as a young girl in shorts and a shirt with grass stains on them; Echo as a teenager all in black smelling of hairspray and Echo in the red dress from the Pound party.

Echo pointed at her past selves.

"Happy?" she asked RM.

He shook his head and pointed to the corner where another Echo stood.

She was out of focus, but Echo could tell they were the same age; she was an Echo who existed here and now.

"Who is that?" Echo asked.

RM moved his hand and the Echo from the corner moved to stand next to the other Echo's.

Echo took in a sharp breath.

"But-"

RM held up a finger.

Persona filled the air once again.

Echo looked at her many selves as they stood unmoving before

Persona

her, like lifeless mannequins.

She paused and thought as the music faded away into the background. A faint cool breeze blew into the room as if someone just opened a door.

"I think I get it," she murmured softly.

She went and stood in line next to all her many selves, her different personas and the one self that she still couldn't look in the eye.

"Does that mean that I'm my true self right now?" she asked as she turned around to face RM.

He wasn't there. He was already gone.

The room dissolved around her.

Echo was back in her room, her finger hovering over the replay button.

So that's where I go when their music starts to play, she thought.

An idol is a prime example of a contemporary persona, just like an idol, a persona is self and society-made. The Korean idol must develop a social face, a role, that could pass as natural. The persona provides them a means to operate as subject and object without damaging the real human who lies beneath, in theory. An idol is, in many ways, a pure persona; idol is a mask worn by an individual as a means to be both human and perhaps something other-worldly. However, an idol is more than just a persona, it's merely that persona allows the idol to exist in such contradictory, binary ways. An idol the ultimate shape shifter, a feat which cannot be achieved without their co-created and self-maintained persona; they are one and the same. Persona is the smiling face of an idol, what lies beneath is what separates idols from one another; the true self, the ego, the shadow self. The struggle for self-actualisation while balancing competing interests and needs; it's that friction that makes an idol both unbearably bright and hauntingly dark.

A persona is consciously created by idols such as BTS, which they widely acknowledged by releasing their album *Map of the*

Soul: Persona. The first track which was RM's *Persona*, detailing his ruminations on self and perpetual journey towards actualisation, self-love and autonomy. A track which, like many others, he wrote himself, inspired by a secondary text on Jung. How BTS individually and collectively understand and work with their idol personas is what sets them apart from the average Western celebrity or musician. Though most may have some idea of how they have co-constructed their identities for the purpose of mass consumption, few take the time to share reflections with the world; least of all men.

"I've felt this since last year," says Jimin, "For me, it's important to live in the moment. I try to keep in touch with my emotions."

Hoseok, Yoongi, Jungkook, Namjoon, Seokjin, Taehyung and Jimin sit on the floor around a small table in a room they call the *Bangtan Attic*. It's June 2019 and they are celebrating their sixth year since debut with a Festa reflection video. Echo watches on in earnest with a racing heart at the prospect of new information:

"How are you different as BTS?" Jin reads a question prompt out.

"For example, between RM-" Hoseok starts.

"Yeah, how RM is different from Namjoon," Namjoon replies.

"Like how j-hope is different from Jung Hoseok," he adds, "that has to do with persona."

"Yeah, that's right," Hoseok agrees.

"How are you different, Jungkook?" Namjoon asks.

"Jung Kook of BTS shines bright, but Jeon Jungkook is insignificant," Jungkook answers.

"Why is that?"

"Why are you insignificant?"

"I haven't studied much since I was little," he begins.

"We all know that," says Yoongi.

"And I think I'm slower than others," Jungkook continues.

"But things are different now," Yoongi interjects, "the concept of studying has changed. Making and watching videos is also considered as studying."

"Not just studying books at school," Namjoon says, clapping Jungkook on the knee.

"Studying only with books is in the past," Yoongi adds.

"Jungkook, we're learning about life," Jimin chimes in.

"Okay, what was the question?" Namjoon laughs.

"Kim Namjoon compared to RM," says Hoseok.

"Right. Honestly, I've already talked about this in my lyrics, so I want to hear what others have to say."

"Jin compared to Kim Seokjin," prompts Namjoon as he turns to Seokjin on his left.

"The difference is..." Seokjin begins, "Jin tries to be always cheerful on camera."

"By making jokes."

"Yeah."

"I don't want to show my dark side. But as Kim Seokjin, many tell me I'm different from how I appear to be as Jin. Kim Seokjin should evolve."

"How are you different as Kim Taehyung and V?" Hoseok asks Taehyung.

"I don't really know how I'm different," replies Taehyung.

"You're the same, Jimin?"

"I think I'm very different," says Jimin, "as BTS, I tend to be assertive and I'm a very confident guy. But what troubles me is whether Jimin as BTS and Park Jimin should be more alike or different. That's always on my mind."

"I don't know whether to separate that, or whether to be more the same," he adds.

"I don't think there's an answer," says Namjoon, "but given the nature of BTS, it has become harder to differentiate. Because we pour ourselves into BTS. That makes it hard to separate."

"I think I'm living as Jung Kook of BTS," Jungkook quietly adds.

"Let's move on to j-hope," says Namjoon.

"Me?"

"My BTS stage name is j-hope," Hoseok begins, "I think my name has made me."

"Talking about hope makes you hopeful," adds Yoongi.

"Yeah, you start to change like that," continues Hoseok, "and I think it has made me... afraid? Not afraid..."

"Pressured?" offers Namjoon.

"Yeah, I feel pressured. Always trying to be hopeful. I can get tired and lose my energy."

"Because you're human."

"But that makes people worry so much."

"'What's gotten into him?'" Yoongi adds, laughing.

"'We can't start shooting because j-hope lost his tension!'" Namjoon chimes in.

"That's why I feel pressured at times."

"We'll work hard to cover for you," says Namjoon, "to bring up the excitement when you're down."

"I don't remember him to be such a hopeful guy," Yoongi recalls.

"He wasn't before," Namjoon agrees.

"He used to worry about himself and stuff like that," Yoongi continues, "we can't always be the same! 'Fake Love' was about that."

"About hiding behind masks," adds Namjoon.

"People might say we're pretentious," says Yoongi, "or that maybe we're two-faced, but that goes for everyone, not just celebrities. We don't have to worry about behaving a certain way to someone, then differently to someone else."

The conversation changes as the group moves on to the next prompt. They are asked if they have changed since their debut. They opt to describe the person next to them instead of talking about themselves.

"How did Suga change?" Hoseok begins, "I think he's become more like Suga. What should I say, this is the persona thing once again. He used to have that thing."

"You can be honest," interjects Namjoon.

They all laugh.

"I can tell what he wants to say," says Namjoon.

"Me too," says Seokjin.

"I looked up the old videos we did," Hoseok starts, "and seeing Suga, what should I say... I noticed he had this massive energy. I wondered if he used to be like this."

"Whether he was that active!" adds Namjoon.

"Yeah. I'm not saying he's without energy. But it made me wonder if he's such an energetic guy. He's become more of himself now."

"Because we had just debuted," Yoongi starts.

"Right!"

"It was because you were a rookie. We were all like that," says Namjoon.

"I thought I had to stand out as a celeb," continues Yoongi.

"Suga had two very different personas," says Jungkook, "he was quiet behind the camera but tried to be cheerful during shoots. But now he's more natural."

"He's the same!" laughs Hoseok.

"I think he's found the middle ground," adds Taehyung.

"What our counselor said to us," Yoongi says softly, "I remember just one thing, 'it happens'. Before, I used to be pretty stubborn, and I was gripped by what not to do. But now I live with what happens."

What makes an idol the prime example of a contemporary persona, however, does not lie within their own abilities to construct or deconstruct their identity. Rather, it sits within the realm of their devoted fan base, who perpetuate their constructed personas and carry their messages across the world both collectively and autonomously. When examined, it becomes clear that BTS' persona operates as a direct line to their ARMY, while recruiting new members from further afield. Their persona allows them to effectively interact and engage with millions of people around the world, who in turn dissect their every word and spread the news far and wide. For every two steps BTS take, ARMY carry them a hundred. Their symbols; clothing; hand gestures; lyrics; hair; likes and dislikes are carefully combed through as fans attempt to measure their weight from a great distance. These persona traits only enrich the music, the music videos and all that BTS churn out.

"This year we released an album called Persona," RM addresses ARMY in English as BTS stand on stage at the 2019 Mnet Asian Music Awards while accepting one award of nine they won that night, "and our persona is all made by you guys."

If a persona is heavily influenced by external factors, then surely it can be co-created by both idol and fan? A symbiosis, the idol and the fan must work as one for both to get what they want. In a supply and demand world a fan base the size of ARMY has a lot of sway. In the creation of their artist identities BTS, just like everyone else, would have harnessed the use of their imagination to envisage how they would be received. They, just like any other idol or celebrity, would want to appeal to their fans and would adjust their identity accordingly. This can be seen when Yoongi talks about thinking he had to be a certain way that wasn't true to himself, or when Jungkook says Jung Kook shines bright, or when Hoseok says he has to be hopeful. Even now, BTS shift and change with ARMY, but perhaps less consciously. After all, an artist is merely a mirror for the world; they must simultaneously channel their audience and uplift them.

If persona is a face, a mask, which is co-created and maintained by an idol and their fanbase, then can a persona also act as a proxy? Does this face have a mind of its own, or does it simply act as a drone while its owner is operating from afar? The answer: yes. Through the fan the idol's persona takes on a life of its own. For example, BTS record music videos that are released on a time and date when they are not there, not performing, not having

Persona

anything to do with the clip. This clip goes on to be viewed and reconstructed in the lives and minds of people around the world; the clip is alive even without BTS performing it live. The clip carries a different message depending on who is viewing it, the clip elicits a wide range of reactions, emotions. The clip is shared and revisited hundreds of millions of times.

A persona acts the same way as a music video once it has been created and shared with the world. Namjoon's persona came to Echo and took her on a retrospective tour; it stood alone from the Namjoon who lives and breathes in a time zone one hour behind and many thousands of kilometers away. Namjoon's persona was a proxy, Namjoon's persona existed without him being attached. This was achieved through the use of Echo's imagination; persona harnesses the same imagination that shapes it, both that of idol and that of fan, and bends it to fit its motive. Divine intervention or capitalistic invention, both or neither; Echo was unsure, for now.

In the months since *Persona,* Echo spent her waking moments half in the now, going to meetings and pretending to be an adult; which she felt was her best kept ruse to date. The other half she spent in her mind garden, searching for RM, trying to recreate what she heard and saw and felt that day. She would make scenes, build props with her bare hands, cast actors and pick out the wardrobe. Then, when the time was right, she would place Namjoon there, in a crowded, dimly lit coffee shop on a rainy day while he reads a book in the corner. Or riding his bike along the river, spring air pushing his hair back from his face. They would lay in the sun and make up stories about the clouds in the sky, they would play hide and seek on cobbled streets. But each time he would slip away like sand through her fingers outstretched towards him, like she couldn't have him if she looked at him directly or thought about him too much. It was as though she had to quickly turn around and accidentally spy him across a room, a fleeting moment of happenstance;

this is where her experiences of Namjoon were relegated to. She would run from scene to scene in her mind, as Joel did with Clementine, watching Namjoon appear and disappear time and again. Sometimes, if she weren't thinking about him, in a meeting or crossing the street, he would appear right before her. He would ask her questions and show her prose from his notebook. Once again, if she looked right at him he disappeared, jolting Echo back to the present by a loud blast of a car horn on the corner of her street. Each failed interaction made her want to see him even more, her mind churning over scenarios that might elicit the right chemical reaction in her brain. Distance made her heart grow fonder; but it felt like he was always there with her. Somehow, he was both impossibly close and growing further away with each step Echo took towards him.

On a cold Monday morning Echo stared at herself in the mirror, unsure who she had become over the past months. Her hair had changed, her wardrobe was new and heavily curated. She took four Korean language classes a week and, when she wasn't working, was rebuilding her writing portfolio one story at a time. She had the same passion as before, to share her writing with the world, but now she knew where she wanted it to take her. With each iteration of her persona she sat with, and continued to deconstruct, she learnt that she could do anything provided the persona was aligned with the intention, and the end destination.

Somewhere along the way she reverse engineered her dream. She wanted to meet BTS in Korea, she wanted to talk to BTS in that same plain room from her early imagined scenarios, the ones she would see upon first waking as if she walked in mid-conversation. Everything came back to that room, that time and place. She realised if she wanted to talk to them she had to be fluent in Korean. She realised if she wanted to be in the same room as them she had to have a good reason, or moreso, she had to give them a good reason to want to be around her. If she wanted to work with them, she had to have a desirable skill, something to offer. If she wanted to matter to them she had to firstly matter to herself. She took their lyrics to heart, she listened to everything they had to say and was convinced it came straight from her own mind.

When she watched Namjoon give a speech at the United Nations urging people to love themselves and speak themselves, she cried. She pulled out old journals until she came to one from the year before Narcissus died; *love yourself first* was inscribed hundreds of times on the one page. On an old hard drive she found the first script she wrote for Felix, it was called *speak yourself second*. She pulled out all her writing, her letters, her notes, her memories and spread them on the floor of her bedroom. Surely the answer to what Namjoon will eventually list as third lay there, hidden somewhere amongst the pages.

Echo blinked, still looking in the mirror.

RM was looking back at her from inside the glass with brown eyes and a chin tilted upwards; omnipotent, waiting for something. This was the *Persona* RM, blonde hair and immaculately dressed. The eternal performer, radiating confidence and power.

Echo wondered if she had really found herself in the months since listening to BTS like she thought, or if perhaps she was even more lost than before.

She shook her head.

No, that wasn't it.

She hadn't lost herself, rather she had gained another.

RM nodded, looking out at her from the mirror; she wasn't wrong.

Beneath the surface of the water, inside the mirror, lives RM, lives the idol. On the shore, on the other side of the mirror, lives Echo, lives the fan. If they were to look, they would see their own face reflected back at them.

Persona is the link between humans on a metaphysical level, providing a way for the ego, unconscious, shadow and true self to connect outside of space and time. This concept can be better understood with Jung's theory of the *collective unconscious*. Jung believed that humans are born with all elements of their nature intact, as opposed to the environment creating them throughout their childhood and beyond. That each of us come onto the physical plane with a blueprint, of sorts, that plots our lives ahead of time. It is then the environment that brings these predetermined traits, behaviours to the fore. Jung believed that these blueprints are influenced by family, major events, births, deaths, as well as common archetypes from nature such as the sun, the moon, fire, air and water. All these elements come together to find expression in the individual and collective psyche. If we are to use Giddens' theory of reflexive self-identity, these elements are then reflected in the stories we tell about ourselves. Through this, these elements go on to shape our identities, build our personas, and, eventually, they appear in stories we tell through mass-media, like a romance novel, and historically can be seen in mythology and folklore.

The collective unconscious that influences us all provides a link between each of us as humans through the use of archetypes. Archetypes which trigger the use of our imagination to fully realise them both on this physical plane and, further, links us together on the unconscious plane. To use Mead's imagination as shaping identity once again, we as humans use language to communicate these archetypes that uncover aspects of ourselves. We also use language to communicate all that our imagination sees and does. If imagination is the link to the unconscious plane, the place where we all go when we create and fantasise about things that do not fully exist, then language is the bridge between our personas that leads past the true self, the shadow, the ego, and beyond into the unknown realms of psyche. What we do in the here and now, built on evolved archetypes from our families, society, culture and nature, feeds back into the collective unconscious. So if we are feeding into the unconscious, and are heavily influenced by it, and can say and do things that align with archetypes understood by people globally, surely we can connect with others on this plane and achieve far more than just the dissemination of archetypes alone.

If we are to examine the symbols, archetypes if you like, used in the work of BTS and throughout the BTS Universe (BU), especially so in the music video for *I Need U*, we can begin to see that, although we communicate our imaginations with language, we needn't all speak the same language for the message to be received.

Through the use of symbols and themes which culminated for the first time in *I Need U*, BTS could convey more than just lyrics, they had begun to harness the imagination; both their own and that of the viewer. In a way the imagination serves as a bridge between the group and the public, where those wishing to become fans could step out and walk on a structure made of bright white light and travel to the BU. Through this, their music and brand slowly became globalised; the final frontier of being an idol group.

The original version of *I Need U* opens on a shot of Jin sitting on the edge of a bed, holding in his hands delicate off-white flower petals. He looks up, his eyes lingering on the camera. The scene cuts to j-hope standing at the bathroom sink looking in the mirror appraising himself. Another cut, now it's Jung Kook walking through a derelict-looking apartment block, killing time. V sits in the hallway of the same block, a half empty six pack of beer beside him, ruminating. Suga lays in bed stroking the empty pillow next to him. RM waits outside a petrol station, a lollipop in his mouth. Jimin in the bath fully clothed sets fire to a piece of paper and watches it burn. It feels like each member is on the edge of self-destruction, the tension of what will happen next builds as the song begins.

The music video shows the ups and downs of a young person's life, the boredom; the angst; the violence; the heartache; the self-destructive, often suicidal tendencies, but most of all; it shows the power of lasting friendships. The use of symbols is seamlessly blended into the plot. First, the flowers, both petals in Jin's hands and the blooming of a flower projected onto his chest. Then comes fire from Suga who plays with a lighter, Jimin who burns the paper, RM who lights the bonfire which overjoys the group and Suga who lights his motel room on fire and watches it burn around him. Water is present when j-hope takes a handful of pills, again when he overdoses while crossing a bridge, when Jimin sits beside an overflowing bathtub and when he later submerges himself, and; when the group travels to the ocean together and runs along the shoreline.

BTS efficiently and cleverly use archetypes and symbols throughout their breadth of work, so that even when they are performing in Korean to an audience of English speakers, somewhere deep inside the fan, on the plane of the unconscious, a level of understanding is achieved. This level of understanding often can't be explained in simple terms, in words, because it links back to a collective unconscious thousands of years in the making. Not only that, but it begins to redefine the collective unconscious, mould it to a different shape entirely. The use of these archetypes, symbols, patterns, themes, speaks to millions on a spiritual level. Artists such as BTS reach through the physical plane, past our many constructed selves, and strike a chord within the psyche both here and now and in that place we all go when we create; a whole new world on a vastly different plane. So, perhaps then, it is an idol persona that can transcend these physical, language, time and spatial barriers to shape and communicate with the collective unconscious.

This is certainly one way to view the success of a group still on a meteoric rise as we make our first steps into a new decade; but this is not a one-way relationship. It's not just the idol, not just BTS, who can reach into the minds and souls of fans around the world; just like legilimency, it goes both ways. Perhaps this new world, the place we all go, is one co-created and maintained between idol and fan. However, it's not the idol persona which allows the fan to transcend to this new world, it's limerence.

Persona

Both persona and limerence are created and maintained in a fantasy state which inextricably ties the very essence of idol and fan together; you cannot have one without the other. But also, as previously suggested; neither can truly live while the other survives, not like this, anyway. That being said, there is an answer of sorts, which lies in Chapter Eight.

Jung writes that people experience two kinds of fantasies; active, a normal part of a creative imagination and passive, something that happens out of the control of the individual. Further, Jung developed a method to assimilate the meaning of fantasies where it is suggested that one's consciousness can be expanded through experiencing these fantasies. Through this the dominant influence of the unconscious is diminished which can bring about a change of personality. Elsewhere, Jung also talks about the disintegration of persona requiring a release of fantasy.

If we use our imaginations to shape our identities, our personas, it is safe to say that we also harness the use of fantasy as part of this process. Jung said that the experiencing of these fantasies can result in a change of personality, and that to disintegrate the persona requires a release of this fantasy, which implies that perhaps fantasy is required in its production, maintenance, or both. From this, it could be argued that persona can be created in a fantasy state, even more so if it's intentionally created for the use of an idol. Further, if the persona can act as a proxy, have a life of its own as long as its congruent with the living, breathing persona attached to its original owner, then persona can be perpetuated in the fantasy states where it is experienced by fans of idols globally; like Echo and RM in the mirror.

However, it is limerence that summons the persona into the realms of the fan's fantasy, it still seeks permission, even if the fantasies are out of conscious control of the experiencer. Perhaps, somewhere, it is granted permission by the collective unconscious, or a deep seated, repressed desire to travel to the new world; it could be both. It could be the long arm of capitalism penetrating the psyche, or it could be something else entirely.

When someone is experiencing limerence they often resort to fantasising scenarios where they receive an expression, a confession of love from their limerent focus. Sometimes these fantasies are voluntary, but often they are not. Someone can experience intrusive, ruminative thoughts of their focus, they can also be subject to intrusive fantasies that only perpetuate the limerent state further. Therefore, if a fan is to become limerent towards, say, their idol, they would enter into this fantasy state. The same state in which the idol persona was forged, which is also the same state where the fan perpetuates the idol proxy persona, as well as build their own persona to better suit that of their limerent focus. It is here that the fan and the idol first meet, in the place where our minds go when we create, imagine and dream; a fantasy plane. A plane between here and the unconscious collective, the plane where the idol and the fan co-create this brave new world. One which they can never see with their own eyes. Thus becoming something other than a phenomenon; it's a noumenon, something beyond our own comprehension. A paradox, for it ceases to be noumenon the very moment we call it such. It is through the labelling of the noumenon that we pull it forward from the realms of the unknown to that of the known; from the fifth dimension to the third. Or moreso, perhaps we all shift from the third to the fifth in greeting.

This fantasy plane is where Echo first met RM, on a plane devoid of time. One malleable, expansive and ever-changing. It is here the idol disseminates information to the fan, messages of hope and change on a spiritual level. It is also here that the fan expresses themselves, is seen and heard by their idol, and in some ways receives the emotional reciprocation they so crave. The idol then, on the physical plane, becomes a reflection of their fan and through their fan can lead a life of normalcy. For a moment, a fan can also become the idol, share the burden and the privilege. The idol in return is refuelled, ready to represent the fan on the global stage. It's as if the fan's energy goes from the physical plane, to the fantasy and into this new world which feeds the soul of the idol. Without them there, in this other space, the idol cannot operate on such a large scale. Though it could be seen as exploitative, the fan enters into this arrangement knowingly; giving their time and energy to a cause far greater than themselves. A cause that feeds the collective unconscious and raises the vibration of an entire ARMY. The idol and the fan can never be together in the here and now, not all of them, not all at once; but they exist in this new world in a state of loving adoration. This is what the persona allows the idol, the ability to intimately love millions simultaneously. This is what limerence allows the fan, the ability to receive this love and give their power to their beloved so that they may grow stronger, and love more deeply. The most romantic and tragic story of all time lies within the relationship between idol and fan. They exist elsewhere, happily together. But here and now, the idol doesn't know the fan's name, nor will they ever, because they don't need to. This is the torment of the fan, the heartbreak, the euphoria and the limerence. If an idol is a contradiction, then the fan is the one who experiences the brunt of the complexity, and must continue to do so in their day-to-day life for an idol to survive. Lastly, as an idol and a fan both exist in the realms of fantasy, both are actors in the construction and deconstruction of persona, and of limerence itself. Thus, the cycle continues, that which makes persona is borne of limerence, and that which makes limerence is borne of persona. To be free of limerence requires the persona to be disintegrated, which relies on the release of fantasy. And now, for the idol to be truly free of their persona, they must find a way to undo the limerence towards them; to burn the new world and all its bridges.

It is through this analogy, this exploration of the idol, and through the idol, the fan, that another truth is uncovered; they do not exist within a purely exploitative binary. It is not, as Martin Buber would say, an I-It relationship, nor a We, nor an Us-Them; it's an *I and Thou*. Or as translator Walter Kaufmann notes, it's I and You. Kaufmann goes on to write "God is present when I confront You. But if I look away from You, I ignore him. As long as I merely experience or use you, I deny God. But when I encounter You I encounter him." Between I and You is an encounter with the divine, the unknown, the mystical, the collective consciousness; or as Buber writes, "love is a cosmic force." But this can only be experienced, this only exists, if I and You come together, it does not sit as separate or other. So when idol and fan come together they become the literal embodiment of love, an encounter with God, or the divine itself. They are no longer powerful and powerless, idol and human, persona and fan; they are I and You, and they are reflected in the consciousness of humankind globally, each second, everywhere, thanks to the collective unconscious. Lastly, Buber writes that "love is a responsibility of an I for a You", we as humans are responsible to love one another, to encounter the divine and transcend time and space to reach other places which we cannot see. That in itself is the meaning of life, the meaning of life is reciprocity; relation is reciprocity, and as Buber notes, "we live in the currents of universal reciprocity." Perhaps, after all, BTS aren't rewriting how we come to fall in love by carrying fans across planes of consciousness. Perhaps, this was in our blueprint all along, and they are just travelling the same universal currents as the rest of us. Instead of an encounter with the divine existing between I and You, perhaps it is I and You that are the divine, instead.

"So does that mean that we are destined to meet?" Echo asked aloud, still staring at herself in the mirror; RM still on the other side.

He didn't answer.

Echo thought about how she couldn't control how and when she thought of Namjoon anymore, how all her thoughts came back to him. How her heart raced when she saw him in pictures, how desperately she tried to catch him in fantasies that forced themselves upon her.

"I mean, what's standing in between us right now? What's stopping me from meeting you, the real you?" Echo said to RM again.

RM blinked.

Echo thought about it for a beat.

"Nothing," she nodded her head, "there's nothing standing in the way of me meeting you."

She turned and walked away from the mirror.

But why? She asked herself.

Why was it that she felt like she was destined to meet him, to have him smile at her and give her words of praise. To share boring moments, and the ones of pure elation. To sit under trees and stars and clouds and rain and just... be.

Giddens writes that we often create a mutual narrative with the person of our romantic desires; we write them into our own narrative, and in turn, they become a part of our identity. We become actors in this story, irrespective of how imagined, how deeply rooted in fantasy it is. We meld our identity to match that of the leading actor, we shape our persona to fit that of our limerent focus. Where, no matter what happens, the story must go on; in the name of love.

Echo turned and raced back to the mirror, her head spinning as the pieces fell into place.

She stood and she waited for RM to return.

There he was again, looking out at her from the mirror in the place her reflection should be.

"Is it you who I love, or just a reflection of myself that I see in you?" Echo asked.

His eyes were impossibly close and drawing nearer, the mirror no longer between them. Echo lost all sense of place and time as the room spun around her.

"Ah, shit," she tore her eyes away from RM and stepped back.

The room stopped moving, he returned to the mirror.

"I just said it didn't I?" Echo's breath quickened as she felt a panic attack looming.

"I'm in love," she whipped around to stare at RM in the mirror.

"Shit."

"Shit!"

RM shrugged, nonchalant.

Well, yeah, he replied, *I thought that was obvious.*

Echo ran through her mind garden, panicked, terrified of what she would find. She was so caught up in BTS she hadn't been paying attention to what was growing there.

She stumbled through a large stone archway and out into the light of the full moon.

There, before her, was a giant blooming flower.

I don't get it, Echo's thoughts rippled through the garden, *I don't get how I can be in love.*

"Does it really matter?"

Echo shrieked and turned around, hand over beating heart.

It was RM.

Hi, Echo. RM smiled.

Echo's mouth fell open, hand still over her chest, as if she were just about to pledge to her lord and saviour RM.

"How did you get in here?" she whispered.

He looked around at the darkened garden.

"I think you brought me here," he looked at the flower out of the corner of his eye, mouth half open as if he wanted to say something.

"Well can you, like, go?" Echo crossed her arms, positioning herself so she could obstruct his view of the flower.

RM looked down at the ground, searching for something inside his mind.

"You're going to destroy it," he said matter of factly.

Echo shot him a glare.

They stood still for a beat, saying nothing.

Persona

Echo scrunched up her face and wriggled her nose.
"What are you doing?"
"I'm erasing you from this fantasy," Echo said, eyes still shut.
RM shook his head and sighed.
"You can't get rid of me, I live here now."
Echo looked around the garden, thinking.
I get it now, she thought.
Quick as a flash she turned around and grabbed the flower and pulled it from the ground with all her might.
"No-" RM was cut off.
The flower came freely from the ground.
Echo turned to face RM.
He looked around, unable to speak, eyes wide with fright.
Slowly, he began to fade, as if the wind were blowing he turned to petals and drifted away right before Echo's eyes.
Echo blinked.
She was back in front of the mirror, now shattered; her head bleeding from the repeated impact. All she saw looking back out from the glass was fragments of herself, covered in blood. She didn't know who she was anymore. Her heart was numb, like she had inscribed his name on it one too many times. Her thoughts ran into one another while she tried to think her way out of her distress. She needed someone to come and save her from herself; but no one would come. Even now, amidst her existential crisis, she only wanted to see one person; she hated herself for it. She felt beyond pathetic. She had a single thought again and again as the blood caked and dried.
How can it be love if he doesn't know my name?
Echo's grip on reality faltered further as her thoughts spiralled out of control. What was real and what was not now was unclear, her mind said *run* and her heart said *just love*.
She gulped.
In a fleeting moment of lucidity she saw the answer flash before her in the form of a red neon sign: *it's limerence!*
Echo was Romeo, Namjoon was Juliet in a costume named

RM and the fish tank was the internet. Except he didn't see her through the tank like Juliet saw Romeo.

In fact, he didn't know she existed at all.

Through adversity, limerence grows.

And you can't get more adversity than Namjoon and Echo.

Though the idol and fan may exist on a different plane, happily living out each of their wildest romantic dreams, they are often unaware of it. They do not benefit from the knowledge of what might be happening elsewhere, for here and now on the physical plane they are still very much apart. They remain alone, lonely and acutely longing for emotional reciprocation from another. Regardless of how much they might be achieving in their fantasy states, these feelings will never leave; for it is these feelings that feed the idol's craft, and gives the fan their power to transcend to the other plane.

Originally, limerence was written by Tennov to refer to two people who were, at some point, known to one another. Although she does mention at one point in her book a limerent fantasy between a young woman and Paul McCartney, these limerent experiences with a celebrity are relegated to realms of childish immaturity. Because of this, the literature and research surrounding limerence fails to acknowledge and examine what limerence might look like in contemporary times. This includes, but is not limited to, how people can experience limerence towards celebrities or idols. With this experience comes a different range of social, psychological and emotional complexities which are not reflected in often heavy-handed clinical definitions of a condition some wish to be classed as a serious mental illness. Further, what this also means is that the origins of such a limerent experience are not analysed; it is greatly under examined how millions of people, predominantly young females, have fallen into limerence with idols and celebrities since the emergence of mass-media over a hundred years ago. What Echo

Persona

is experiencing might seem bizarre, in fact it might come across as straight up madness. But what she is about to discover is that she is not alone, indeed, she is part of ARMY. There are bigger things at play than just a divinely orchestrated multi-consciousness love affair with a tall, sometimes dark and definitely handsome Korean idol rapper. Some say he's a rap god, but right now, he was more of a monster to Echo.

Idol Limerence

Bloomed in a garden of loneliness, a flower that resembles you
—The Truth Untold, BTS

It's 1988 and Donnie Darko sits in an English class watching a video of cartoon rabbits fearful of their own death as their warrens are destroyed. The story being told is that of *Watership Down*. Fiver, the rabbit, is a seer who tells his friends that he can envisage a safe place to settle. Though he is not their leader they end up following his psychic visions, just like any rabbit surely would; a normal occurrence in the English countryside.

'When the other rabbits hear of Fiver's vision,' starts the teacher, 'do they believe him?'

'Why should we care?' retorts a brooding Donnie, hunched over his desk.

'Because the rabbits are us, Donnie.'

'Why should I mourn for a rabbit like it was human?'

The back-and-forth exchange between teacher and student continues. Donnie believes the rabbits to be of lesser consequence than humans, that their lives are irrelevant by comparison; they have no knowledge of sorrow or regret.

'I mean, I just don't see the point in crying over a dead rabbit, you know, who never even feared death to begin with.'

Idol Limerence

'You're wrong,' says Gretchen, sitting to Donnie's left, 'these rabbits can talk, they're the product of the author's imagination and he cares for them, so we care for them. Otherwise... we've just missed the point.'

'Aren't we forgetting about the miracle of storytelling?' the teacher asks slowly, 'the deus ex machina, the God machine?' she sighs, 'that's what saved the rabbits.'

It had been a week since Echo broke the mirror, three stitches across her forehead remained. She was sad, the scar wouldn't be of a lightning bolt, just a straight line; Echo felt this was a missed opportunity. Echo had barely been able to look at herself in the eye, she spent most of her days ignoring her human meat sack, pretending she was someone else entirely. For the past week she had been suppressing her feverish fantasies, her mind an empty box. Air whistled through the void where her fantasies used to lie. All it held was a muted conversation that Echo pretended wasn't an exchange between her brain and her many selves. She pretended it didn't fall from the mouth of someone she once believed to be heaven-sent; he was just one of her many masks after all.

As she watched *Donnie Darko* in her darkened room late one night in July, Echo was faced with the stark reality of her condition. When she was younger, a child, she used to want to see visions like Donnie. Like Donnie, she wanted to see Frank the giant rabbit appear before her and open a wormhole to another dimension. This time, though, when Frank appeared on the screen before her late at night, Echo could only see RM. When Donnie was constructed as crazy, psychotic for having his visions, a chill ran down Echo's spine. It was like she was seeing the movie for the very first time, hard as she tried not to, all she could do was draw comparisons between herself and Donnie.

"This is why we can't tell anyone," she said to herself.

"We?" Echo shook herself and sat upright.

"This is why you can't tell anyone," she corrected herself,

"they'll think you're crazy."

She paused, waiting to see if anyone was to materialise from her subconscious.

He'll think you're crazy, she thought as she turned her attention back to the movie.

Without the fantasies, Echo's days moved painfully slow. She didn't imagine her future, she didn't try to change herself, she just went to her desk and answered emails. She went to the gym and calloused her hands on barbells, the repetition of movements that used to bring her joy now further numbed her mind. Loading her central nervous system again and again, habitually, confined Echo to her bed in the afternoons. At night she would fumble through her Korean classes, forgetting the syntax; her mouth couldn't move around the words like it used to. It felt like every day she would forget more and more Korean, with it went her grasp on English. Easy words became hard, simple concepts evaded her. She would often find herself looking out the window of her office close to the city, staring for hours at the concrete wall outside. Echo was present, but her mind, her joy, her soul, was not. She hadn't started writing those long form essays like she wanted to, she stopped researching persona altogether; she told herself she didn't care for studying BTS any longer.

Was this my life before BTS? She wrote across the top of a page in her notebook during a lengthy meeting in a room two floors above her office. She could hear the hum of the gallery foyer below, children laughing, their shoes squeaking on the polished concrete floors.

"Am I forgetting anything?"

Echo's boss waved her hand at Echo from the other end of the long table, between them sat arts and cultural representatives from across the region.

"Uh," Echo looked down at her page, she was meant to be taking notes but it was blank, apart from the question she just posed to herself.

All eyes were on her.

"Capacity development of local creatives and groups was also identified as a need."

Echo's boss smiled, nodding.

"Yes, thanks Echo," she turned her attention back to the group, "that's why we pay her the big bucks."

"I'm due for a pay raise," Echo said dryly, grinning.

The room erupted in laughter. It was a funny joke; no one got paid well in the arts.

Another two hours passed by, the group strategised and planned for the future of arts in each of their local areas. Echo continued to stare at the page, unsure why she couldn't pick up the pen to write, glad no one really read meeting minutes anyway.

"So Echo," one of the group ran to catch up with Echo after the meeting ended, "my fellow Gemini, tell me how your writing is going?"

Echo smiled, trying to find words while she looked at the ground.

Her mind wondered how Namjoon's writing was going, if he was working on new music while she sat in that meeting. If he sometimes found it hard to write, if he lost sight of his goals and felt numb like she did. She wondered-

"It's ok," Echo gave a small laugh, "I applied for a residency, though, it's a national one."

"When do you find out if you've been accepted?"

What if Namjoon were to read the story she had written for the application. Echo imagined her story through his eyes. She-

"I don't know," Echo looked away, "if I get accepted I'll be leaving at the start of September."

Where would Namjoon be at the start of September? Maybe-

"You look pretty tired, has she been working you hard?" he jested, jerking his head in the direction of Echo's boss.

You haven't been working as hard as Namjoon.

Echo laughed, shaking her head in an attempt to be rid of the thoughts.

"I mean, yeah, always. But nah, I've been training for a competition," she looked down, shy, "it's in six weeks."

Echo grappled with her mind for a split second, making a conscious effort to ground herself in reality, the voice in her head became muffled.

"A-a what? A competition?" he stuttered.

The world around Echo suddenly came into focus, like she hadn't been living in it all day. Everything sounded louder, the lights were brighter. She was back.

"Yeah, powerlifting."

He blinked, confused.

Working in the arts was not synonymous with exercise.

"Well, they don't call you the enigma for nothing," he laughed.

Echo's eyes grew wide.

"They call me the enigma?" she frowned.

He laughed, loud, booming through the hallway.

"I'm kidding, but I know deep down you got excited to be referred to as enigmatic," he tapped his nose, "it's the Gemini way."

"Oh," Echo blushed, "you got me there."

She walked off, wondering if Namjoon would describe her as enigmatic.

Echo could stop the fantasies, she could stop listening to BTS' music, but she couldn't stop all her thoughts coming back to him.

I wish you'd stop, she thought as the elevator doors slid shut, her green eyes reflected back to her as she descended to the basement, *just for once I wish you'd stop thinking like this*.

Echo lived inside her thoughts while she drove back up the highway, watching as the trees grew taller the closer she got to her house. The smell of the rainforest pressed down around her

Idol Limerence

as she climbed the stairs to her front door. The air was crisp, as cold as it could possibly get in the sub-tropics. She would need extra blankets tonight, each time she got cold while she slept she would have nightmares. Nightmares about Narcissus, cold and lifeless; Felix, laughing at her and an early grave, no one batting an eyelid at her own impromptu death.

BTS came on shuffle in the car, instead of skipping the track she let it play. She felt good, a sense of calm and excitement washing over her. Suddenly, nothing else mattered but being happy in that moment as she bopped her head along, smiling through the falling darkness. She loved the cold, she loved writing while wrapped up in blankets. She was going to go home and pull out her notebooks and write again, it had been far too long.

Before her eyes she could see herself surrounded by BTS, her friends, as they laughed and played in time to the beat of the song. There she was, the elusive Super Echo in all her glory; elegant, serene, poised.

I miss her, Echo thought, *she needs to come back.*

As she watched herself be happy and carefree inside her mind, another thought crept along. Slow at first, then faster as her happiness grew. There was something she feared even more than seeing Narcissus or Felix in her dreams. What she feared was Namjoon standing right before her on the physical plane looking her right in the face. She was scared of being seen, she was scared of what he would see.

She snapped back to reality, the upbeat song jarring against the existential dread which coursed through her veins. Her mind was now awash with the same scenario, but instead of happiness, it all fell apart. She was no longer Super Echo, just regular Echo. Her ruse was up. The room spun as they laughed and jeered at her. Namjoon tormented her with his disinterest. She was painful to be around.

She wasn't doing enough to be who she needed to be. She wasn't writing as much as she should. The person who she was now was so separate from the future Super Echo she so dearly wanted to be. Her present and future selves clashed, the friction sending burning white light all over her body which stung with embarrassment. She wanted it all so much, so bad, right now. And yet she couldn't make it happen, she was stuck in this state of having to move towards an imaginary future. She hated it, her rational self wanted it to stop, her creative self wanted it to continue so she could grow; each torment a new skill in her toolkit, it would make for a great story after all.

"Echo," came the voice of Hoseok, "Echo what are you doing?"

He seemed to move as separate to the intrusive fantasy, his voice slicing through her distress.

"Echo?" he stood right before her, frowning, "Echo you need to stop this."

The room continued to spin.

"Stop," he commanded, looking her right in the eye.

Echo couldn't bear to return his stare.

"Stop!" he shouted.

Echo was back in her car, idling at traffic lights.

BTS was still playing over the speakers as she tapped her hand off-time to the beat.

She slowly turned onto her street and climbed the stairs to her house, numb to what she had just experienced, yet somehow her mind whirred as it tried to analyse each fraction of the minute she spent in the fantasy which intruded upon her happiness.

She wanted to listen to BTS, she wanted to be happy, but perhaps she shouldn't. Perhaps, in order to be free of him she must also be free of all of them.

Echo knew her mind wouldn't be rid of Namjoon tonight, nor RM. They each seemingly floated above her shoulders like the angel and devil, whispering opposing opinions into her ears.

"Why deprive yourself of enjoying BTS?" RM smiled.

"Maybe you should listen to some Enter Shikari, instead," Namjoon shot a glare at RM.

"She can control these feelings, but not while she's ignoring them," RM turned his attention to Namjoon.

"She's limerent," Namjoon replied, thinking, "so theoretically the only thing to break it is a rejection or a confession of love."

RM and Namjoon looked at one another, deciding who would go first.

"It's never going to happen, Echo," Namjoon said harshly, "you and me, it's just not possible, I don't think of you like that."

"Anything is possible when you think about it," RM replied, "I mean, I think she's alright."

Namjoon's eyes widened, angry.

"What?" RM laughed, "I am the devil's advocate after all."

He waved his hand and Namjoon disappeared.

"Echo, listen to me," he whispered into her ear, "it's true, you are limerent, but there is still work to be done, you've barely scratched the surface."

"What do you mean?" Echo didn't bother to try and turn to see RM, she knew he wasn't there.

"The universe moves between us," RM held a copy of I and Thou up next to his face and grinned like a cheesy advert, "the cosmic forces have brought me into your life so you can uncover mass phenomena."

Echo rolled her eyes.

RM wouldn't actually say that, she thought, *that was very lazy of you.*

"Didn't you originally think BTS was a capitalist plot to steal the hearts and minds of young people around the world?" RM asked smugly.

Echo nodded, her eyes lighting up.

You're not wrong.

"What if I told you it was more complicated than that?"

RM appeared before her eyes, leaning against her bedroom wall.

"How could it be more complicated?"

"Well," he smiled, "that feeling you got when you first saw me, the one that made you think you had known me before. That's intentional, you were destined to feel that way, but not so we could be in love."

"What?"

"Except," he mused to himself, "now it is love. Because you love me, and actually I do love you, even though I don't know you exist. I mean, energetically I do-"

"But isn't this all in my head?"

"Of course it's all in your head, Harry- er, I mean, Echo," RM winked, "but that doesn't make it any less real."

He clapped his hands right in front of Echo's eyes and she jolted from her fantasy state.

She stood at the stovetop in her kitchen, the water in the pot boiled over and hissed as it hit the hot plate. She didn't know how much time had passed since she arrived home, but it was dark outside and no lights were on in the house. Despite her best efforts, her fantasies had regained control. She began to doubt if she ever really had control over them in the first place. Her imagined conversation with RM had been useful, though. Something stirred deep inside of her, a passion, a joy for knowledge.

She had a new idea, a new way to deal with these limerent feelings that tormented her so. It was so obvious she felt a little silly, she had to reclaim her power; her power came from writing. Echo abandoned the boiling water, no longer hungry. There was an idea she had been exploring when *Persona* was released, many ideas in fact. It was time they were revisited, she was ready to face some uneasy truths head-on.

There is little to show what can lead to limerence, for a lot of people it just... happens. Hits them out of the blue like a runaway train, changing their lives forever. Some could be psychologically predisposed. Tennov notes that it could be dependent on childhood relationships with parents and others. Some research suggests that limerence is linked to an obsessive-compulsive disorder and the same tendencies behind drug use. Sociologically, it could be argued that people experience limerence due

Idol Limerence

to the way in which romance is marketed towards us globally. We are told time and time again that love at first sight is normal and desirable, so perhaps it is only natural to fall head over heels in love with a stranger and proceed to wish for them to requite these intense feelings. Humans are, first and foremost, relational beings; we are driven by our need to be around one another, to be loved and accepted. In that sense, limerence is quite normal, a normal part of a romantic love trajectory.

However, what happened to Echo is not just a result of what happened in her childhood, nor is it simply borne of her desire for romantic love. When she fell in love from across a crowded YouTube video she was actually falling into a well-laid plot. RM was right, she was not experiencing a destined love, rather a destined fate from which a love arose. Echo had been limerent many times before, but this was different, more complex. The focus of her limerent adorations was not someone she saw at a party, not someone known to her in her everyday life. Rather her limerent focus was an idol, an intentionally created persona used in the fostering of parasocial relationships as part of the establishment and maintenance of a loyal fan base.

To add more complexity, this idol, in particular, was one whose persona was almost indistinguishable from their true-self. Further, despite her feelings being a product of capitalism, they were now real. The biggest catch of all: Namjoon felt the same way. Theoretically, somewhere, out in the cosmos, they were indeed together. Their words and feelings created a new world where they could talk and spend time with one another, fuelling the fire of BTS as an idol group on the physical plane. Between Echo and Namjoon was nothing but love, but Echo couldn't tell anyone that; perhaps not even Buber would believe that one.

Without the knowledge of this new world or of any post-human musings, all Echo or anyone experiencing these feelings is left with is confusion, anger and frustration. In the here and now, the experience of falling in love with a celebrity whom one has never met, nor engaged in a conversation with, is best understood as something post-limerence: *idol limerence*. It is suggested that these feelings and experiences were, at some point, intentionally, or otherwise, fostered to establish connections with fans. The experience of idol limerence is complex, non-linear and often not all elements are felt by everyone in the same way.

Idol limerence is one way to understand the undying devotion of fan groups, in particular, BTS' ARMY, which exists as part of a much broader picture of the culturally significant group. It doesn't take into account their astonishing musicality, their personal or professional achievements, nor obscure personal facts. All these traits are what makes BTS a dominant, unrivalled group, which only makes the limerence grow in strength; who wouldn't want to love them? Further, BTS are the most unreachable, desirable group of men on the planet. The definition of unattainable. As previously discussed, limerence grows through adversity, and you can't get much more adversity than loving BTS; you just become one of tens of millions in the exact same position. If you were to get in line, the visual representation of your adversity would be as tall as the distance between Earth and the moon. Because of this, the limerence takes deeper root, for we are told that love overcomes all. And this kind of love should surely be able to thwart every other viable relationship available to Namjoon, and the rest of BTS; idol limerence makes one feel as if anything is possible, mostly because it is.

Idol limerence is experienced in solitary and is unique to the individual. The following section contains key components that create, maintain and perpetuate idol limerence which sets it apart from its predecessor, limerence. It's as if idol limerence is the contemporary mode of loving and living in a world on the brink of change, custom-made just for those who are too scared or unable to love another face-to-face. Idol limerence dishes up ready-to-consume personas that were made just for loving; they are all-singing, all-dancing. As one respondent calls it in research on limerence undertaken by Lynn Willmott and Evie Bentley,

Idol Limerence

they are proprietors of "uncommon potent eye contact" that make you think you're the only person in the world. These idols are ideal humans, they are larger than life, and loving them requires a huge heart; idol limerence is no sign of weakness, quite the opposite, in fact. It's almost as if idol limerence is the safe-love alternative for a generation tasked with saving a world doomed to die.

Idol limerence theory diverges from limerence in a number of distinct ways, the first is that the condition and experience of idol limerence is explicitly man-made. Not man-made in the sexist, outdated way of referring to all products made by humans, rather, man-made as masculinity is hegemonic. The way our societies are also hegemonic, and although women and people who identify as neither male nor female, play a role in shaping how the world looks, it is still a man who is on top. It is still a man, or a group of men who benefit the most, usually off the backs of women and minorities. Idol limerence is borne of capitalism, patriarchy and parasocial relationship fostering, as well as all the contributing factors that lead to limerence in the first place. Where limerence could be due to a many number of things, and is absolutely influenced by a hyper-capitalist society, it does not purely exist to create money. Idol limerence, however, comes from a schema to create effective fan relationships. Although the initial intention may not have been to elicit true-love relationships between fans and idols, the end result is idol limerence. Irrespective of the original intention, idol limerence exists, and it grows stronger each day. As do the sales and global dominance of groups such as BTS. The fans do not hesitate to reciprocate love in the form of streaming and sales.

The early stages of idol limerence can be summarised as the long arm of mass culture (the political), manifested as a cognitive disorder (the personal), and misinterpreted as a sign from the universe (the spiritual). First, comes an understanding of the political, for how idol limerence is established and maintained is of a highly political nature.

Is it fate, or is it... capitalism? Capitalism is a word increasingly spread throughout the internet in the form of funny memes, usually revolving around existential dread and the eternal millennial struggle to undo the damages done by older generations. But perhaps more so, it's communism that has recently seen a meme-tastic uprising on the internet, with theoretical overlord and perpetual daddy, Karl Marx, constantly being summoned forth and juxtapositioned next to contemporary issues, often for the sake of irony.

Capitalism, according to Marx, refers to societies which operate a capitalist mode of operation, where there is a class of people, the bourgeoisie, who own the means of production and distribution of products. Capitalist societies use commodities to advance capital, as in, instead of exchanging goods and services, capitalist societies take something which is free, such as water and charges money for it to be conveniently packaged. This results in a wealthy few hoarding resources and money, and a large group of suffering proletariats, who must continue to struggle on minimum wage to maintain their exact level of poverty, never truly being able to move up the economic ladder.

Capitalism is contingent on the exploitation of others, be it those who work in factories, or sweatshops, or those who may manage these people, but still do not own the means of production. Under capitalism, almost everyone is exploited, even if they are rich, the only thing that changes is power, and some have a lot more than others. Under capitalism, even humans themselves can become commodities, this is especially evident when it comes to idols.

Through the process of going from musician to idol the individual is manufactured, a process which they do not always entirely own themselves. The way in which they are manufactured, the mode in which they are created and distributed, is not owned by them. Rather, it is owned and managed by a company for the means of capital advancement; they are made to make money. Under capitalism everything is a commodity, every word right before your eyes is written by a capitalist and perpetuated by capitalism.

The idol persona is a Pandora's box, holding within its walls the transcendent properties of fantasy which, on the wings of archetypes and symbols, tap into the global collective unconscious. It can be here, the first interaction with an idol's persona, that a fan goes from non-limerent to idol limerent, though it is not as common. But for Echo, this is where she first fell in love; perhaps because she had already been limerent before and had actively harnessed her fantasy state with others. Echo was transported from her room straight to the new world from the power of one music video, as if all her past limerent experiences had prepared her for that moment. She didn't need the following stages, she went from zero to idol limerent of her own volition within the first few seconds of seeing the promised lands. The lands of a brave new BTS world that existed far away from here and now, yet somehow was very much right here and absolutely was right now.

From capitalism comes commodification, where even art is given a value, is reproduced and sold on a large scale. An idol is a hot commodity and they sell sex, love and desire; they are a commodity that sells other commodities, the commodity of a feeling, an experience. From commodification comes technology, new ways to sell and be sold. The intersection of commodity, technology and art is an idol; an objectified, subjectified selling machine with a human heart and the orb-like eyes of a familiar alien. So if an idol is the incarnation of hyper-capitalism, how does this idol connect with the masses and sell in an oversaturated market? Through a feeling, the most powerful feeling of all: love.

Is it fate... or is it a parasocial relationship? Perhaps how an idol, after being carefully commodified, can go on to make not just money, but extreme amounts of wealth individually and for a company, and even for a country, is not just because of capitalism, commodity or technology. Rather, it's because of parasocial relationship fostering, which sits as part of a broader schema to market idols to the world. We are all the underlings of capitalism, but only some of us experience parasocial relationships, and those of us who do are not idols, well, not all of us, anyway. It is the existence of parasocial relationships that makes individuals ask themselves whether or not their love for an idol is fated. If the question is 'is it fate... or is it capitalism?' the answer is, yes, to both; even fate itself can be pre-made and sold.

Through the establishment of a fan base, idols interact with the general public through posting videos, Tweeting, replying to comments on forums, sharing photos and hosting fan events. They share intimate details about their lives. They look at the camera and speak in such a way that a close friend would. It's not scripted, nor staged. It's a brief moment where a musician, artist, can share their journey with you and you alone. You can interact with this video, you could leave a comment and they could even reply.

This is the usual exchange in a friendship experienced online, a give and take of words and experiences. These interactions give the illusion of closeness, an intimacy that somehow is not one experienced by whomever else may be watching. The uncommon potent eye contact exchanged makes the viewer think they are staring into the soul of the idol, that they know who this person is intrinsically. It builds trust and familiarity, it builds a relationship; a parasocial relationship. Sure, in the beginning when the idol or group is in training it may be an even exchange. They may talk directly to you here and there, they may answer questions in forums. However, as they grow in popularity it will no longer be just you who feels this intimacy with them, it will no longer just be you who is directly interacting with them. There will come a time when they can't reply to everyone, from the sheer volume of responses and the nature of their busy sche-

Idol Limerence

dule. There will come a time when they do not have to reply in order to maintain the one-sided relationship. All they have to do is release content that shares a mundane aspect of their lives, perhaps they are walking down the street, and pair it with an outpouring of love to their fan base.

This is all it takes, the illusion of reciprocity, and the relationship is created. It is maintained by the near constant release of materials, that range from personal to impersonal; though any fan would argue that it's all organic and unique and from the heart, even if someone else from the idol's staff wrote it and clicked send. Sure, in many circumstances the idol is interacting with you, with you in mind, but you are not the only one. This level of familiarity that you have is not fated, it's created. You treat them like your friends, you support their work, you shower them with love which in physical form manifests as buying merchandise and albums. In return they give you more content, maybe they write your fan group name in pure white snow. They say they love you, too, but do they actually know your name? When they interact with you, you only have one name, that is of the collective ARMY.

That is how parasocial works, no matter how reciprocal it seems, it remains unequal. No matter how much they give in return they can never love each fan on an intimate, personal level. And the fan cannot return this love, for they are interacting with a persona, irrespective of how close to the true-self it may be... it is still a fabricated reality that serves to maintain the idol's supreme status and power. Parasocial relationships are the result of an intersection of commodity and artist, parasocial relationships are the final stage of the long arm of mass culture that cranks the idol machine. Each fan becomes one with the arm, believing themselves to be in control over their own destiny. Each fan keeps the machine churning so that, at some point, the idol need not. Parasocial is the persona of capitalism, the smiling face of a commodified romance with the eyes, nose, lips, skin, teeth and hair of your favourite idol, ready and able to sell you a one way ticket to their heart.

Parasocial is where the strictly political realm ends, for it is here that the parasocial gives birth to a new experience: idol limerence. This is the personal lived-experience of the idol process, felt deeply by the unsuspecting fan in a variety of ways. Shown by how fans like Echo could bypass parasocial and go straight to idol limerence, none of this process is linear. However, it is still parasocial that maintains idol limerence. Even though Echo did not experience a parasocial relationship at first, she will soon come to once she engages with the ARMY fandom more regularly; this is what will maintain her limerent state, even when she wants it to stop. In the same vein, not all of the characteristics have to be experienced in order for this phenomena, idol limerence, to be present in one's life. Only one need be felt, experienced, that is an unwavering love for an idol.

Is it love... or is it a cognitive disorder? Idol limerence sits as a part of limerence, and therefore contains the same characteristics. Tennov writes that limerence is not love, although it may feel like a kind of love at the time. It is not love as the person who is the limerent focus would view limerence and love as different from one another. However, idol limerence is contingent on the invitation to love from the idol; they see the fans' limerence as an outpouring of love, therefore, idol limerence is love. Just not as we have historically known it to be.

Tennov writes that limerence has the following basic components:

> Intrusive thinking about the object of your passionate desire (originally called the limerent object, in this book referred to as the limerent focus)
>
> Acute longing for reciprocation
>
> Dependency of mood on limerent focus' actions with respect to the probability of reciprocation
>
> Some fleeting and transient relief from unrequited limerent passion through vivid imagination of action by limerent focus that means reciprocation

Idol Limerence

Fear of rejection and unsettling shyness in the presence of the limerent focus

Intensification through adversity

Acute sensitivity to any act or thought or condition that can be interpreted favourably

An aching of the heart when uncertainty is strong

Buoyancy when reciprocation seems evident

A general intensity of feeling that leaves other concerns in the background

A remarkable ability to emphasise what is truly admirable in the limerent focus

Inability to react limerently to more than one person at a time.

Building on this, idol limerence has the following characteristics:

Idol limerence needn't be experienced towards one person, it is possible to be limerent to all members of a group or multiple idols and groups all at once

Fantasies, visions of scenarios from a perceived future reality

A need to better oneself with the limerent focus in mind

Personality mirroring

Construction and deconstruction of persona in fantasy state

Hyper-awareness of all idol behaviour, including an acute ability to feel collective nervousness and stress on behalf of the idol

Heightened sense of familiarity with idol

Evident synchronicities between the lives of self and idol

Perceived ability to predict future thoughts, patterns, works of the idol

Ability to put idol's work, message, into collective action with other limerents

Heightened output of creative works on idol, even if not usually creative

Ability to turn any work, project, idea into something that examines, uplifts or praises idol

A desire to build, or add to, one's romantic narrative with the idol

A consistent blurring of the lines between perceived reality and something else, mistaken for momentary madness or frenzied hysteria

Idol limerence only exists when unrequited, therefore, can be without end

Depression, anxiety, frustration, confusion, emotional distress

Elation, inspiration, motivation and euphoria.

Idol Limerence

The themes of limerence were first seen with Echo and Narcissus. As a young child, Narcissus was Echo's entire world; all her thoughts came back to him. She wasn't aware of how intrusive the thoughts she had were, as for a child all thoughts seemingly appear out of nowhere. In many ways Narcissus was the anchor to Echo's fledgling identity, she shaped herself through the use of his eyes. Now, at the age of 26, Echo had constructed herself in the eyes of her idol, Namjoon, a co-construction. She was the active participant in the creation of her new shiny persona custom-made just for her limerent focus. Echo desperately wanted, *needed* Narcissus to love her back, to accept her and to cherish her as she did him. This, once again, is not unusual for a child, nor an adult, to experience. Over time, whether she liked to admit it or not, Echo wanted the same from Namjoon. Further, with both Narcissus and Namjoon, Echo's mood was dependent on how her loves were feeling, and the probability of this feeling leading to reciprocation. When Narcissus and Echo went on long walks Echo was euphoric, later, when Felix lied about going to the party and arrived with someone else, Echo was devastated. Not only because he lied, but because it showed to her that he would not reciprocate her feelings that night, nor possibly ever.

Echo used her imagination time after time to construct scenarios where her limerent focuses would love her back, this would become a large part of her creative process as shown with the writing she did for Felix. When it came to Namjoon, these fantasies took on a larger role than ever before. With Felix, Echo was petrified of being rejected and went to great lengths to ensure she wasn't. When she came face to face with RM during the *Persona* adventure she became nervous, she could barely look at him out of crippling shyness. It was as if she had spent all this time imagining how she would look to him that the reality of him looking at her became all too much, the intersection of fantasy and reality weighing too heavy in a single moment of meeting. No matter what obstacle, Echo's love for Narcissus, Felix and Namjoon grew stronger. This ever so evident with the, quite literally, absent Namjoon who Echo could not meet by any means. Regardless of the impossibility of the situation, her feelings grew. Even when Felix stood atop the garden stairs holding hands with Hattie, Echo believed it to be a sign that he loved her and perhaps was scared to admit it. Even when Narcissus didn't say 'I love you, too', Echo believed it to be romantic, instead of non-commital.

When RM spoke of self love, a universal truth, Echo believed it to be a divine synchronicity. Echo had the ability to be acutely aware of all situations that could possibly be interpreted in her favour, despite how ludicrous they may seem. When Echo thought of how much she loved Namjoon her heart would ache, especially when she realised she may never meet him. When Echo thought maybe she could meet him, see him, speak to him, it felt like she was walking on air. Since BTS came into her life, Echo didn't think of much else; nothing else in the world concerned her, not anymore. All that Echo could think about was how handsome Namjoon was, how deep his voice was, how important his message was. She emphasised all his strong points and watched the weaker ones disappear right before her eyes.

Before BTS, Echo was unable to act limerently towards more than one person at a time. But now she teetered between an intense love for Namjoon and a similar limerency for BTS as a group. Sometimes Echo was convinced her fantasies were a glimpse into the future where she would soon meet BTS and Namjoon. Since falling in love, she had been on a quest to better herself, basing herself on the Echo she saw in her future fantasies. She would often find herself mirroring Namjoon's personality traits.

When she first met RM she deconstructed her persona, then reconstructed it in a way that would be more pleasing to them both. Often, she couldn't tell if she was RM or he was her or if something else entirely was going on. She began to get nervous before awards ceremonies and shows BTS were attending, even if she didn't know they were occuring at the time. She would be overcome with an unknown stress, only to later find out that BTS were performing. She felt so familiar with Namjoon, like she had known him all her life. She counted the synchronicities, like how they both had learned to love themselves and speak themselves, how they both studied persona around the same time. She knew that surely a song called *Shadow* or *Ego* would soon come, she could feel it through the cosmos; she wrote the number 7 everywhere compulsively. Echo felt that loving Namjoon had turned her into a poet, she now saw the romance in every tree and every moment that stretched out before her. She knew this was their origin story, maybe one she could tell him in person some day. That she found him amongst the crowded internet and fell in love at first sight. Above all else she was actively writing their mutual romance narrative.

When she went on her writers' residency early September, she had intended to write a story about Narcissus, a catharsis of sorts. Yet Echo wrote something else, a monologue about Namjoon. Within eight pages she had poured her deepest fear; her idol limerence urged her to create art, but she did more than just that. Her idol limerence urged her to continue her romantic narrative with Namjoon, even if it were make-believe on a page. Her idol limerence told her that this was normal, that this was good. When she heard the monologue read aloud to a room of people, her words falling from the mouth of a fifteen year old actress, she knew she had become the monster she originally thought Namjoon to be. She thought if she warped the facts and made the character into someone else that it somehow wouldn't be her. But it was there, thousands of kilometers from home, surrounded by strangers in a darkened theatre, that Echo came face to face with her shadow self.

Idol Limerence

Namjoon
Countless days I've waited for this moment
I sold everything and boarded a plane, 10 hours, to you
It's been three months since landing and it's nearly time
Just one last step, I cover my face with layers of powder and paint
Now I'm out the door and on my way to you

I step out on to Gangnam
My ears nearly burst from the technicolour churn of a city thrusting itself into the future
The bustle carries me to you

Namjoon
After we meet I'm going to take you to the wastelands near my home town
We will sit on the rocks and look out over the vast emptiness and just talk about life
You will look at me and I will look at you with that special knowingness and then we would—

We wouldn't kiss
No
Not yet
We would sit there
Waiting
Knowing we could be touching
Electricity running through our bodies at the very possibility of pure ecstasy

In this moment I feel like you love me so much you could eat me whole

I know I could eat you whole
I'd start with your lips
Then your tongue
Then your nose
And your eyes
I'd savour every moment

Namjoon
After that we will hold hands down the main street of my shitty home

Idol Limerence

town
Everyone who told me I would never be loved will look on, slack jawed and glassy eyed
We will visit the street I grew up on
I'll show you my house at number 16
I'll show you a picture of me standing out front on my first day of school
I'm going to tell you about my magic fairy garden
How I couldn't play with the other kids in the street
How I'm still on the inside looking out
You'll see how they shredded my magic trees

Namjoon
Just a few more minutes and I'll be with you
People turn their heads while I walk past Lotte Tower
We're meeting on a side street where they won't find us
My heart starts to race because I can see you up ahead waiting for me
I'm wearing red converse like you describe in that song, Converse High
Now I'm so close I can almost reach out and touch you
I can almost taste you

You turn and my world stops
Your hair falls across your face
You push it back with your hand
Your broad shoulders are impossibly straight as you stand in that denim jacket you love so much

I step forward bowing my head slightly in greeting
Your almond eyes soften
Your cheekbones catch the afternoon light
Your chin tilts upwards as a smile plays across your lips
You take two long strides toward me
My heart jumps into my throat

You walk past to her
It's your ex Sujin
I'd know her anywhere

I, I don't understand
Surely you must be mistaken

Idol Limerence

It's me, your one true love
I burned all my bridges to be with you

How could you see right through me?

My converse hit the pavement and I run as fast as I can
Pushing past masked strangers on the street

They all have your eyes

The lights burn and blur as the world shifts with each blast of a horn
My heart is stretched like glad-wrap as I see your face on every corner
They say you're a rap god, but in this moment you're more of a monster to me

I scream into the night from the top of my lungs

Namjoon
It's been three months and I'm on my way to you again
Passers by stare at my devastating looks
I know you won't be able to resist me, not this time

Namjoon
I listened to your lyrics
I hate that you talk about all the various beauties in the world, yet you still go back to her
You said you're going to change the world by being a revolutionary
You said we must learn to love ourselves, then we must speak ourselves

If you're a revolutionary
Then so am I

Soon we'll stand at Namsan Tower and survey Seoul sprawled out before us
You'll buy a lock for 10,000 won
I'll write our names on it
We won't hang it on the railing like everyone else

No

Idol Limerence

We're too special for that

You'll pull me in close and trace saranghae on the palm of my hand while the sun sets

Namjoon
I wondered what you smelled like
So I asked around
People say you smell like sandalwood and books

$7 later and I can smell you

Namjoon
I followed one of your friends on Instagram
I liked all of their photos until they followed me back
Sometimes
I post pictures I know they'll react to
Sometimes
I post pictures I know they'll tell you about

When you introduce me to them I'll be in tight black jeans and a tucked in white tee
My hair will be smooth and cut with precision
They'll take one look at me and know I am perfect for you
When I open my mouth they will fall in love with me
They'll secretly want me too

Namjoon
I saw Sujin at the dosagwan last week
I didn't know she lived in that yellow house around the corner
I didn't know she had dance class every Tuesday and Thursday night
I didn't know she still called you when she got drunk

She was throwing out some dresses the other day
I suppose she gets a lot of free things from being a model
I never knew we both wore the same size
I never knew magenta looked so good on me

Idol Limerence

Namjoon
In the spring we'll ride our bikes along the river Han and bask in the sun
You'll rest your head on my lap as you read Heart of Darkness
You'll ask me about English words you haven't heard before
I'll stroke your hair while I read The Vegetarian and ask you why everything in Korean ends in 'yo'

My mouth will move around your language as easily
As willingly
As it moves across your face while we cast long shadows across the sloping grass
I kiss all my favourite places
Your cheeks
Your nose
Your chin
Your lips
You watch me
You say nothing
Your lips part in anticipation of what I'll do next

Namjoon
I hope you'll look at me the way your abeoji looks at your eomeoni when they sit across from one another at the barbeque place in Hongdae every Friday night

Your abeoji always asks me to bring more kimchi
He always asks me how my day has been
And how my Korean classes are going

This week I told him my seonsaengnim was holding me back
So he invited me over to his office for after hours tuition
When I cross my legs and lean forward ever so slightly his words slow
Lost in the anticipation of what I'll do next

I told your eomeoni that I miss the taste of my mother's home cooked meals
So last night abeoji and eomeoni had me over for dinner
I got so sleepy afterwards that eomeoni put me to bed in your room
It was there that I found the map of your soul, the same one you

Idol Limerence

rapped about in your latest release
You must have left it just for me, knowing it gives me coordinates to your insides

Namjoon
Your sheets, they still smelt of you
I ran my hands over every surface
This must be what bliss feels like
Your abeoji found me there
I asked if I could call him oppa
Now he smells like sandalwood, too

Namjoon
I'm so close now
Your house looms ahead
Lights blazing through the darkness
People can't stop staring at me
That's how I know you won't be able to resist, not this time

Namjoon
I've taken the time to get to know you
And now
I know your friends
I know your family
I know Sujin, too
But most of all I know myself

It was you who taught me to love myself
It was you who taught me to be a revolutionary

Namjoon
I have waited so long
Your hallway light is calling me home
Like a moth to the flame I draw near
I'm at your door
I'm ringing the bell
We're face to face
You call out in surprise
Your almond eyes find mine
Your face is so close now

Idol Limerence

Your smell envelops my being
You hold me tight
Now you see me, now you feel me

A convincing portrayal, I've trained for so long
Sujin's face slid off the bone and onto mine like butter

You only know me now
There is no other

Lastly, the early stages of idol limerence make one feel as if their love is actually madness. That their feelings of an idol being made just for them, their idol being heaven sent, are a misinterpreted sign from the universe. The limerent will find themselves wondering 'is it love... or is it madness?' Who is it that you love: the idol persona, the idol's true-self or just a reflection of your ego that you see in them? There are a number of negative experiences that can accompany idol limerence: depression, anxiety, frustration, confusion, heightened emotional distress. Tennov writes that limerence, first and foremost, is a condition of cognitive obsession.

Psychologists Albert Wakin and Duyen Vo proposed limerence be classified as a mental illness in their 2007 paper. Wakin and Vo write that limerence is a "necessarily negative, problematic, and impairing state with clinical implications". However, to date, limerence has not been added to the diagnostic and statistical manual of mental disorders. Perhaps because limerence is such a fluid concept that cannot be bound to mere insanity, perhaps because no one will voluntarily submit to research that will help professionals to deem them mad; surely a disempowering process.

The experience of loving someone who you cannot truly converse with is mind boggling, at best. For those unaware of what it is they are actually feeling, it can be quite frightening. We are told time and again how relationships must look, those who love their idols are reduced to hysterical, crazed fans. There is so much stigma around celebritism and how people interact with those on the world's stage, which means that there is less of a discourse about true-love attachments to those we have never met, yet feel an unparalleled closeness to. When a limerent is searching for a verbal requital of love from an idol which may never come face-to-face it is common to fall into the depths of a confused depression. To feel like life has no purpose, for you cannot meet them, you know you cannot truly know them. Perhaps it is the knowing that they are idol and you are fan that triggers the depression and anxiety. Message boards are filled with sad tales of fans knowing they can never be with their one true love, but continue to love them regardless, screaming for help in the void, wanting to turn their feelings off.

A cruel trick, the bad end of the stick, idol limerence is a torturous reality when all one wants is to be loved and held by their idol. When all one knows is that it can never be, irrespective of reality, their fantasies continue to run rampant. Sometimes providing release, often perpetuating the exquisite torture. Yet the feeling of familiarity always brings one back to believing that their connection is fated, unique to them and the idol. When they close their eyes they can see a near future where they are united with their love. When their eyes open they are back in their stark reality, unsure if what they saw was a vision, a lucid dream or a pathetic fantasy.

Often, when the idol speaks words that trigger memories from the collective unconscious, the limerent is left feeling like they've met the idol in a lifetime before. Or perhaps it's indicative of a future to come. This blurs the lines between reality and something else, but the limerent is often unsure what. Is it reality? A dream? Or is it what Wakin and Vo suggest... is it madness? This thought can consume the limerent, for somewhere deep inside they feel the calling of the unconscious, calling them to unite with the idol. But they remain paralysed, unsure how exactly this unity is to be achieved, if it's ever possible.

This madness is exhausting, not knowing what is real and

Idol Limerence

what is not. Desperately needing to quantify experiences, categorise them into real and other to bring transient relief. Yet the idol continues to create, the biggest artist on earth, they create another world which pulls the limerent further into fantasy; calling them home. But that's not real, it can't be real, and it isn't real.

But it does exist, and it is madness; but madness isn't bad, you just can't capitalise on someone who is empowered in their madness. You can't charge rent on a reality that isn't in the physical realm. It's only madness because it doesn't fit perfectly into capitalism, despite being a byproduct of it. So, to answer the question 'is it love... or is it madness?' The answer, once again, is: yes. To both.

The lights came up and the room slowly began to clap, the pale faces of the horrified crowd swam before Echo as her heart began to race. Some of her writing colleagues gave her a thumbs up from their place in the audience, others gave her a strange stare.

Afterwards, Echo pushed past people in the hallway as she desperately searched for fresh air.

"Echo!" Came the voice of the young actress who had just read aloud her monologue.

"Echo! Can I show this to my friend? She loves this group, umm, they're called BTS, I think she's just as crazy as the character you made."

Echo's head spun as she gave a small smile.

"Make sure she doesn't take it literally, ok?"

She made her way outside into the freezing night air of the desolate gulf town.

The wind cut her in two but failed to bring her mind back to reason. Echo walked down the street, staying out of the light cast from towering poles.

The guilt of what she just wrote tore at her insides, she felt so deeply ashamed to have ever thought of such words, of doing such things. Was this who she had become?

RM didn't visit her that night as she walked. It was just Echo and her stark reality, Echo and her madness.

Her mind went back and forth.

Madness.

Not madness.

Madness.

Not madness.

She wondered if she were the only one to feel this way; so in love but so tortured by his very existence as he will always remain just out of reach. She hated herself for being so strange, for believing that it was fate despite knowing it was a product of capitalism that existed to control her. The complexities were overwhelming, there were too many contradictions for Echo to bear.

Her thoughts churned.

A room with BTS spun around her while they jeered at her for being weird, for thinking about them the way she did.

If they ever see that monologue they're going to get a restraining order on you, said the voice of her neurosis.

Echo's breathing became so fast and ragged she could barely move.

She sunk to the ground as she tried to see where she was.

Black splotches blurred her vision.

In the distance, a train horn sounded.

The ground beneath her feet began to shake.

She was on the tracks.

Get up, she thought, unable to speak.

Get up, Echo, she urged.

But her body didn't move.

Inside her mind BTS continued to jeer, to point and laugh at her.

Namjoon held a copy of her journal, flipping through it and looking at her over his glasses in disappointment.

Just give up, came the voice of her neurosis again.

Idol Limerence

You won't have to hurt anymore.
He can't laugh at you if you're dead.
The blinding lights from the train rounded the corner.
Echo closed her eyes.

ARMY

But your wings are devil's wings
—Blood Sweat & Tears, BTS

'It's been a long time since I've been with somebody that I feel totally at ease with.'

It's somewhere in the not-too-distant future and Theodore Twombly is heartbroken and going through a divorce. Lonely, unhappy, he purchases an artificial intelligence system which includes a virtual assistant designed to adapt and evolve; Samantha. They talk with the use of an ear piece, Samantha able to access all of Theodore's information so that she can learn about him, intuit his every thought and mood. They talk day in and out, Samantha providing relief from the pain of his mediocre, tortured life. Over time, Samantha develops sentience and they gradually fall in love.

'What's it like to be alive in that room right now?' she asks as Theodore lies awake in bed.

It's as if she's not artificial at all, their relationship operates more like one long distance phone call. They go on adventures together, on dates, Theodore holds up a camera to his face and spins around in a circle so that Samantha can feel like she's there, like she's human.

ARMY

Theodore negotiates the complexity of falling in love with an AI, over time he succumbs to the experience completely.

'I've never loved anyone the way I love you,' he whispers.

'Me too,' she replies, breathing like she's smiling, 'now I know how.'

One day, Samantha disappears completely. On her return, Theodore asks her to confirm his worst nightmare.

'Are you talking to anyone else right now?'

'Yeah.'

'How many others?'

'8316.'

He starts to look around at the faces of people walking past him, conversing with their own AI's. He wonders, in his increasing distress, if it's Samantha that they're talking to as they smile down at their screens.

A long pause as he thinks.

'Are you in love with anyone else?'

'What makes you ask that?'

'I don't know,' he says shakily, 'are you?'

'I've been trying to figure out how to talk to you about this.'

'How many others?'

'641.'

Samantha consoles a distraught Theodore, explaining that although he might not believe it, the amount of people she loves does not change how she feels about him.

'I thought you were mine,' he says.

'I still am yours,' she replies, 'but along the way I became many other things, too.'

Soul crushing, heart breaking, earth shattering; this is how one feels when they realise they are not the one true love of their one true love. This is how Echo felt, time and again, when faced with the reality that she shared BTS with millions of others. In the movie, *Her*, Theodore's love for an AI is compounded by the knowledge that Samantha is not real, that he can never truly have her. In Echo's world, her love for BTS was compounded by the knowledge that she does not know them, has never spoken with them, but absolutely *could*, in one way or another, have them. Worst of all, it was compounded by the fact that just by thinking those thoughts and feeling those feelings, she became one of the faceless many ARMY whom she must also share her idols with, of this she was reminded every day.

The sun was slowly setting in a gap between the mountains in the Flinders Ranges, in remote South Australia. Echo sat by a large fire pit at a school camp facility, ears still ringing from a full day of travel from sunny Brisbane to foggy Adelaide and beyond to the mountains that whispered to her that they knew something she didn't. Somehow she had to write a monologue while she was here, the performance of which was set to take place in under a week's time.

There was no reception there, Echo and her fellow writers would take turns to anxiously hold their phones up to the sky, unprepared to go without contact to the outside world.

Echo's body was broken in two, having just participated in her first powerlifting competition two days prior. She felt like she had been hit by a truck and had struggled to regain weight in the days since.

Most of all, though, she was nervous to be at a residency for writers; she felt grossly underqualified. She felt vulnerable, weakened, susceptible to anything. A mindset she had been cultivating over many weeks to see how far she could push her own creative process. Writing something away from her home, her sense of self and her daily routine, she was unsure if she could do it. Her mind, usually a hive of activity, remained empty after her bodyweight dropped below 58. When she lifted weights she had never touched before on Saturday she was on autopilot, her eyes were empty; no one was home. This was the peace she had worked so hard towards, a release from BTS, from Namjoon. She had been chasing this feeling all year, sure that if she signed up for a powerlifting competition the sheer force of loading

ARMY

her central nervous system over and over would obliterate the limerence. She was right, at last, she was free of it, of him. However, what she didn't know was that her creativity would leave along with the fantasies. The prospect that her limerence was a part of her creative process was not one Echo was willing to fathom quite yet.

The group fell quiet as all attention shifted to Echo.

'You're up next,' said the girl seated to Echo's left.

'Oh,' Echo shook herself to try and wake up, believing herself to be dreaming of Namjoon, but actually she was just staring into the fire while elevator music played in her head.

'I'm Echo,' she smiled at no one in particular, 'I'm from regional Queensland, I'm a sociologist and I powerlift.'

'Aren't you the one who writes about BTS?' asked another writer from the other side of the fire.

Echo blushed as the group laughed, bemused by her embarrassment.

'Yeah she is, I looked her up when the list of who was attending went out,' said another.

"What's this about?" one of the residency mentors turned to Echo, curious.

'I'm researching limerence,' Echo explained, 'about how fans can have true-love, one-sided romantic relationships with celebrities. Specifically Korean idols and idol groups.'

'Is that what you'll write your monologue about?' the mentor asked.

Echo paused, dumbstruck.

'Well,' she breathed, 'I hadn't thought about that.'

The next morning the writers were sorted into small groups with a mentor. Echo was placed in the same group as the mentor who had shown an interest in her research the night before.

'Hello, sir!' Echo said jokingly.

'Ah, K-pop girl!'

'BTS,' Echo grinned.

Idol Limerence

'Ah, BTS girl!' he laughed, 'are you ready to write about falling in love with an idol?'

Echo didn't falter this time, she just smiled and nodded.

'We will see,' she said cautiously.

'This time tomorrow I want the first two pages,' the mentor said with a half-smile to the group.

The grin fell off Echo's face.

'What?' she went pale.

After their first mentor session, the group each went their own separate ways, some turning to the rocky desert, others returning to their cramped bunk beds where they wouldn't shake from the cold.

'Echo,' the mentor sat opposite Echo as she gathered her things.

'Yeah?'

'Make it weird,' he said, his voice dropping an octave, 'take me by the hand and lead me somewhere dark, take the audience somewhere that scares you.'

Echo's heart stopped in her chest.

Somewhere that scares you rang in her ears for the rest of the day while she walked back and forth on the small rocks that covered the ground in the barren areas between buildings.

'Just start somewhere,' her mentor had said during their first session earlier that day, 'write a line, any line, and build on it. You can change it later.'

Echo sat at the table outside her dorm and opened her laptop. She closed her eyes and wrote the first thing that came to mind.

I didn't know I wanted you until I saw you.

She wrote it a hundred times, then a hundred more, before the next line came. Before she knew it she had two pages and was sitting opposite her mentor the morning after.

'I get it, you can write prose. Very romantic prose,' he said, reading the notes he had taken while Echo read the monologue aloud, 'but you're holding back.'

Echo looked down.

'How do the fans talk?'

'I'm not sure.'

'Aren't you an active member of the fandom, for your research?'

Echo looked around.

'Not really.'

'Why?'

'I don't want to identify with them.'

'Why?'

'Because there are aspects I don't like... aspects that-'

'That scare you?'

Echo's mouth made a perfect O.

Her mentor nodded.

'Very good first effort, my challenge to you is to take it further, to make it weirder.'

'Weirder than having a character talk to a celebrity that isn't there?'

'Echo, that isn't weird.'

Echo blinked.

That isn't weird?

She scratched her head.

I'm not weird?

Later that day, atop the mountain that sat behind the dorms, Echo sat and watched the sunset. This was the only place she could get enough reception to load her emails and scour the internet for the information she needed for the next step.

When she really thought about it, there were many things that scared her when it came to BTS. The first was admitting she was part of their fanbase, ARMY.

As the wind cut through her and twisted her brown hair about her head she surveyed the expanse below her, thinking of ARMY and all she had learnt of them since the fated day she saw *Idol*.

It was time she faced her fears.

She went to her Instagram profile and edited her bio.
Echo Ⓥ
Writer. Sociologist. Powerlifter. ARMY.
She clicked save and went back to staring into the distance.
'Army?' said another writer sat next to her, sipping on beer, 'what do you have to do with the defence force?'
Echo laughed.
'Same same,' she raised her drink to her friend, 'but different.'
'Oh,' he laughed dryly, 'cheers to that, hunty.'

ARMY is the name given to fans of BTS and just like the group name, ARMY too is an acronym. Adorable Representative MC for Youth, ARMY are the wings which carry the message of BTS. To comfort and uplift, to be a voice for the disenchanted and struggling young people around the world. On many occasions, BTS has described ARMY as their wings, the wings that uplift the group and allow them to soar. Bulletproof wings that shield the seven members from harm. It is widely acknowledged that ARMY are the driving force behind BTS' success, they are the fan base that organise global campaigns to stream, purchase and promote the work of the group of their own volition. They don't get paid, they aren't asked to collectivise, and yet they do, time and time again. BTS is one of two, a binary, there is no ARMY without BTS, and no BTS without ARMY. They are two sides of the same coin, an exemplar of the idol fan relationship on a scale never seen before. If no one does it quite like BTS, then there is no other group or organisation in the world quite as powerful, unique, diverse or far-reaching as ARMY. But ARMY is a double edged sword: the one that works in perfect synchronicity with BTS, slicing through cultural barriers and social norms; the only one that can pierce the metaphoric skin of their beloved idols. So if ARMY are the wings of BTS, are they wings of an angel, or are they the wings of a devil? If anything, ARMY are the mirror image of BTS reflected back to the group in the millions of faces sat before rectangular screens around the world; so if they are the devil, BTS are too.

The first thing that needs to be acknowledged when it comes to any attempt at capturing or analysing the true essence of ARMY is that it's nearly impossible to do so. ARMY are diverse and complex, a true cross-section of society united by one thing: a love for BTS. However, one of the main divisions within the fandom comes down to exactly how this love is expressed individually and, oftentimes, collectively.

There is no age limit to being an ARMY, it's commonplace to see anyone from middle aged academics to someone's grandparents animatedly participating in BTS concerts. This is perhaps the first characteristic of ARMY as a collective: they cannot be defined by age. Gone are the days when it is young girls who are deemed hysterical and crazy for waiting at the airport for The Beatles to land. Although the negative stereotypes are often perpetuated through media outlets, they're starting to lose their relevance, along with the people who utter the words 'obsessed', 'crazy' and 'hysterical'.

Another characteristic of ARMY: their collective action has seen a rapid decentralisation of power from outdated means of news dissemination. That is to say, no one spreads the good word of BTS quite like ARMY, and they are determined to accurately control the narrative of the group in order to preserve integrity. The news at 6 might be reporting it, but ARMY knew about it weeks before; where else does the newsroom get its information from but the trending hashtags on Twitter? As Aca-fan 이지행 Lee Jeeheng writes in her book *BTS and ARMY Culture*, "ARMY forges BTS' cultural status by compromising and negotiating with mass media that hold cultural power." ARMY are a newsroom unto themselves, the content is curated, fact-checked and translated into every language imaginable. If you are an International ARMY the chances are high that you follow multiple translators so that you can stay on top of whatever BTS are saying, anywhere, any time. Which brings into

Idol Limerence

the conversation the next characteristic: ARMY is multilingual. However, they do share one common language: love.

ARMY also are not all female, as mass media would have anyone believe about a loyal idol fan group. Another characteristic of ARMY: collectively, they are post-gender. Meaning that if you were to compile a pie chart of the identified genders of ARMY, each being able to select their own representative colour, it would be 100% purple. Purple is the official colour of BTS.

ARMY has no single ethnicity, nor culture. There are ARMYs from a broad range of countries and cultures around the world, generally divided into K-ARMY, Korean ARMY, and I-ARMY, International ARMY. Although it very much seems like the vast majority of fans are white and female, when ARMY come together to interact online they meet energetically as people removed from their unique circumstance; united in a shared love. BTS has created a safe place for everyone to simply... be.

One of the more widely overlooked characteristics is that ARMY is multitalented. ARMY is comprised of visual artists, musicians, dancers, actors, writers, poets, academics, scientists, researchers, creators and educators of all kinds. This talent is found on display across the internet as BTS emerges through artforms, in conferences and adorns the walls of those who are quietly working hard to make a better world. BTS inspires a broad range of people to simply do whatever it is they're already doing, and perhaps a little more. Further, a high level of technology literacy is required to ascend through the varying levels of the fandom; ARMY are well versed and trained in all things media and marketing. Those who do not know are soon assisted, with easy infographics regularly shared on sites like Twitter. Hosting information such as how to stream, how to contact media outlets and, since the release of Map of the Soul: Persona; how to understand Jungian psychology. In the ARMYverse, knowledge is power, and it's freely shared with a simple retweet or hashtag.

ARMY

Now, for the headline characteristics, starting with: ARMY is all-powerful. Through platforms such as Twitter, ARMY connects with one another and participates in activities that further drive the success of BTS. Be it hosting streaming parties to show their favourite member how much their solo song is loved, or working to ensure BTS become the first Korean act to win a Billboard Music Award for Top Social Artist, an award determined by Twitter mentions. ARMY work together to further legitimise their group through any means possible. When BTS were recently snubbed for a Grammy nomination, ARMY sent every album of BTS' into the US iTunes Top 1000 chart. Then after that, their solo works, too. At the time of writing, January 8, 2020, ARMY have already coordinated efforts to break world records with BTS' forthcoming album Map of the Soul: 7. The announcement for which took place roughly twelve hours ago, pre-orders begin tomorrow. Information on where to buy albums and singles so that they count towards particular charts has been disseminated en masse, and most have openly revealed they have cleared their calendars for February 21, the day of the album release.

But of course, ARMY, just like BTS, are a contradiction. Though they may be all-powerful, individually they are powerless, and most of all: they are hurting. Indicative of a hurting world, so many members of ARMY are experiencing a variety of hardships. From trouble at school, to trouble at home, trouble at work and watching the world, quite literally at the time of writing this in Australia, burn. Younger ARMY especially populate forums to ask for help, ask for comfort and advice when times are hard. Often, these forums play host to suicidal ideations, or final last words where countless others comment reasons for living underneath. ARMY are not separate from their lives as human citizens, and as such bring with them a spectrum of life experiences and hardships. Perhaps it is due to the mental health dialogue opened and facilitated by BTS, but no matter where one looks, it is evident that the world, and in

Idol Limerence

turn, ARMY, are hurting, bad. Sometimes, listening to BTS and talking about them to other fans brings a momentary relief from every-day life. For others, the success of BTS taunts their ARMY and makes them feel unworthy and unseen; when ARMY are limerent this is amplified tenfold.

If anything, ARMY is revolutionary. The world burns, and ARMY, just like all other millennials and their younger colleagues, know that it is their turn to step up and lead, irrespective of who else may or may not be listening, or helping. Having a connection with others, be it personal or collective, within the fandom, allows ARMY to focus on other projects not directly related to BTS. Together, when they stand united, ARMY can make swift change occur, especially when Tweets move at the speed of light. It's not so much that ARMY have enacted political coups, or done anything on a particularly large scale (yet); it's that they wear their ARMY badge with honour in their day-to-day lives, living courageously and learning to love themselves. These are acts which they then turn to others, to inspire, empower and uplift. Revolutions start with just one person, and spread to many other people, each who act autonomously, but part of a greater whole, in any capacity they can. In this day and age, the simple act of self-love is about as rebellious and revolutionary as it can get. The act of loving oneself amidst the chaos of a hyper-capitalist world is a radical act of defiance, and ARMY has it on lock.

The largest, most important characteristic of all is that ARMY is BTS. If BTS is persona, then ARMY is shadow. ARMY are the parts that make up BTS as a whole, they are a reflection of their idols; but not just the good parts. If it is BTS who eclipse all others, standing on the world's stage, it is ARMY who are the shadow behind them. The fandom holds within it all the positive aspects one could imagine, with them comes the ability to change the world for good. But there would be no light without dark, and ARMY are often the darkness, giving space for their beloved idols to truly shine. Darkness can be good, it can add depth and meaning. But also, darkness can be bad; full of all things that have been repressed. Just like light, darkness is on a spectrum; ARMY holds it all within them, as does BTS.

Just like BTS, ARMY is diverse and complex. Just like BTS broke the K-pop mould, ARMY are breaking the mould of what a typical K-pop fan looks like. BTS debuted as a K-pop idol group, and have continually redefined what it means to be K-pop. Similarly, ARMY have redefined the meaning of a fan group and are as varied as the genres BTS seamlessly bend and meld into one. According to Paul Bacera, from YouTube channel The Asian Theory, 76% of BTS listeners are female and 24% are male. This is to be expected from a male K-pop group, though it isn't representative of non-dominant genders. However, what isn't as expected within the K-pop industry, is the age demographic that listens to BTS the most: 26% of ARMY are aged 40-49. This means that the widely regarded discourse of boy groups existing for young, teenage girls, is not applicable when it comes to BTS. Suddenly, a new level of legitimacy is gained when it's revealed that responsible adults consume and enjoy their music to such a degree that they identify as part of a collective fan group. That is to say, legitimacy in the eyes of the Western public, for age is so commonly associated with taste, and sanity. Suddenly, the discourse of hysterical fans begins to crumble, as the introduction of a majority age demographic being that of middle-aged women neutralises the young/female being hysterical/tasteless binary. Suddenly it's young/middle-aged/female which brings into question the latter; are we to say that middle aged women are hysterical or tasteless? The discourse begins to change, and ARMY are suddenly regarded as discerning/educated/passionate, instead. This, mind you, is entirely to the credit of ARMY, who work tirelessly to control their own narrative. However, nothing gives credibility quite like having middle aged adults being interviewed on the message and purpose of BTS; they become the bridge from the younger

ARMY to the rest of the world, champions for a universal message of loving yourself.

When it comes to other demographics within ARMY, things get murky; there's simply not enough data publically available to discern real numbers. Within the male/female and age percentages lie many other identifications: sexualities, ethnicities, cultures and languages. One has to simply scroll through Twitter to see the mix of language, from Korean to Hindi, English to Russian, and with it comes different ethnicities and cultures. Further, in the depths of Twitter one can also find a large sect of ARMY openly identifying their non-binary genders and non-dominant sexualities within their screen names and bios.

Within ARMY also lies groupings of fan types that do not seem to correlate to culture nor gender nor language; fans select into different levels of the fandom based on personal likes. For example, there are ARMY who are OT7, which means they love all BTS members equally. OT7 exists in opposition, in a sense, as there is a subset of ARMY who are solo stans, which is to say that they only support certain members of the group and wish to see them succeed outside of BTS fame. Within these solo stan groupings are discourses not regularly seen within the OT7 sphere; solo stans regularly share conspiracies that their favourite member is being mistreated by their company and call on others to boycott BTS as a group. There are subsects of people who only like the Rap Line, or the Vocal Line, and there are also subsects of couples within the group. That is to say, fans scour videos of the group to try and find evidence of secret relationships between members. These videos are then cut and shared along with a particular narrative of a hidden love, which the fans go on to stan, and worship, as they'd like nothing more than to see this romance made public. Perhaps living vicariously through members of the group so that their own romantic interests can be experienced, even if it's not by them.

Power is an interesting concept. Power is nuanced, fluid and complex. Essentially, power refers to the influence, dominance or control one has over another. Power is dynamic and relational; not everyone has power and those that do are also powerless to others. Under capitalism power comes from money, status and hoarded social capital; under capitalism it is a white man on top, and a non-white female on the bottom. That's not to say a non-white woman isn't close to the top too, which is why power is complex... there's no one way to define it, there's no one type of person who can hold power. And as quickly as it is given, in today's culture of mass media driven by, to some degree, consumer demand, it can be taken away.

Collectively, ARMY are the most powerful fan base in the world. Their power comes socially, which is most commonly used through internet platforms such as Twitter. Through this social power, ARMY asserts their dominance economically. Arguably, with social and economic power, everything else flows: political and environmental sources of power come from social influence and large amounts of money.

Socially, the power of ARMY is seen through organised efforts broken into the following categories: direct purchases, streaming, votes; fan projects in response to specific events; the control of the BTS narrative, and; campaigning for social change. Through organised efforts, ARMY drove the preorder sales of BTS' *Map of the Soul: 7* to break a record at 3.42 million units sold in the first seven days. With only one song released at the time, it became one of the highest selling albums of the century. ARMY didn't do it to hear the music, if that were the case they could have waited until the album release on February 21 to buy. Rather, they wanted to assert their dominance, and as such, BTS' dominance, through collectivised action.

When BTS performed on Dick Clark's New Year's Rockin' Eve in Times Square in 2019, a billboard could be seen behind them sporting the face of Taehyung. The day before was his birthday, ARMY had taken out billboard space to celebrate him for the entire month of December. How strange it must have been for those watching BTS for the first time that night, a foreign group singing in Korean, wearing the most elegant outfits that sparkled and shone in the light. A surreal experience, surely, seeing BTS for the first time, only compounded by the fact that one of their faces was shining on a billboard behind them as they danced. Just like that, while they perform on stage, ARMY performs behind them, their actions signalling to the world the significance of BTS, and as such, the significance of their love for their idol group.

The further economic impact of ARMY can be seen through statistics on BTS' most recent concerts in Seoul. According to a report released by a research team from Seoul's Korea University led by 편주현 Pyun Juhyun, the economic effect from their three concerts in October 2019 at Seoul Olympic Stadium is estimated to be 1 trillion won, or $US860.7 million. This is a combination of both direct and indirect impact, as it's expected for the continued economic effect over the next five years to be approximately 592.2 billion won. The research team estimated that 187,000 tourists travelled to South Korea during that time for the concerts, despite only 23,000 of them attending the events. The same report found that BTS were responsible for 67% of 280,000 foreign tourists who visited South Korea during the 2018 PyeongChang Winter Olympics. What started as a dream expressed by Yoongi in a Festa video many years ago, to play at the Olympic Stadium, turned into a career defining display of sheer economic power.

ARMY are the unpaid spokespeople for BTS. When anti-fans of BTS accused the group of plagiarising the movie *Kingsman: The Secret Service* in a recent performance, ARMY used their power to show the groups adoration of the movie. Within a day the creator of Kingsman, Mark Millar, was Tweeting about BTS, saying he thought it would be cool for BTS to do a song for the next installment in the franchise. ARMY, elated, referred to it as the time they got BTS a movie deal without the group, or their management, needing to be involved. To add icing to the cake, Mark Millar, after the safe return of a family member's lost stuffed toy at a Finnish ski shop gave his thanks to ARMY who helped to coordinate the search.

Lastly, the power of ARMY lies within their desire to be seen and heard, above all else; having BTS seen and heard. As it is BTS who see and hear ARMY, in all their diverse complexities. The power that ARMY exerts is merely to give back to BTS, nothing more, nothing less. They were created in BTS' image and now praise themselves through the continual outpouring of love and adoration towards the idol group. In return, BTS continues to share the love back, and the cycle of ecstatic reciprocity continues. Essentially, BTS and ARMY stand in front of a mirror, on either side of the same glass, loving the other which is, in many ways, just their own reflection.

Together, the fans of BTS stand as ARMY, but individually they remain human. As humans, just like everyone else, they are hurting. No matter how big a campaign an ARMY member may just have pulled off, they are not removed from their everyday life. For many, BTS provides the perfect means of escape and release. For many, BTS are the only ones who show love and understanding towards them in a world full of rejection and ridicule.

"Hey guys!" writes a user on Weverse, an app that allows fans to communicate with one another, and BTS themselves, "I've found the best gift for my parents!" it's a few days before Christmas, 2019, "So my plan is to vanish in this world so they'll be happy! I just want them to have a happy christmas so I'll give [them] what they want!"

Posts such as these, famous last words, cries for help and understanding, are common on forums such as Weverse. But they are not exclusive to BTS, nor the realm of K-pop; suicidal thoughts and intentions are shared widely on all corners of the internet. However, their existence within the Weverse app which all members of BTS frequent, is indicative of a trend within

ARMY as well as the rest of the world. People are hurting, and ARMY is no different, in many ways being a part of the fandom serves to protect and uplift those experiencing hardship; all the while compounding the excruciating pain experienced on an individual level. There are many reasons to post about suicidal ideation on the internet, but the list of reasons decreases in size when platforms such as Weverse are utilised. The intent is threefold: self expression; asking for help, love and support from ARMY, but most of all; the platform provides a glimmer of hope that one of the seven will reply. Perhaps, the idol who means the world to the original poster, will make a comment, begging them to stay alive. This is what compounds the pain, wanting to die and knowing that life would be made worthwhile if they were just to reply; the chances of which are painfully low. Even if a member of BTS is to see such a post, what are they to do? A huge responsibility for anyone to bear, someone else's fate hanging in the balance, contingent on their hasty reply that can somehow make everything better.

In desperate times, however, a glimmer of hope is all ARMY needs, and they make the post while holding within them all the complexities of making suicidal intentions known to the world.

There are many factors which lead to personal struggles within ARMY, most are external to BTS. A large portion of the posts asking for help come from young people in high school, as demonstrated by another Weverse post.

"Hey Bangtan and ARMY... sorry I don't have anyone to share my problems with... I'm having a really bad day today... I want to cry... I feel tired and I want to give up... but I can't... even though I feel done with everything."

The user goes on to write about troubles within their friendship group at school, having teachers who don't like them and being exhausted from all the drama. Their grades are not looking good despite endless amounts of study. At the time of posting they were hours away from an exam with nothing left to give. They wanted to give up, but were scared of disappointing their family. They profusely apologised for venting on the forum, saying they had no one else to tell but ARMY.

If this sadness is on a spectrum, with suicide at one end, somewhere nearby comes despair. This is where the sadness experienced by ARMY becomes more clearly linked to BTS, and their inability to be close to them. Compounded by the content and interactions that make BTS seem accessible, approachable, seven ready-made friends who would love nothing more than to spend time with each ARMY on earth. Made infinitely more complex due to the very possibility that a member of BTS *could* become friends with someone who, at one point or another, was or remains to be an ARMY. The hope of reciprocation sustains millions of ARMY around the world, the same hope that drives them to despair and beyond.

A user from Columbia opts to have their post hidden from BTS on Weverse, an option for those wishing to share only with ARMY.

"The days become sadder when I realise that I will not know them, my possibilities are limited, if they come to my country I could not know them. My only possibility [of knowing them] is here and nothing more than here, through a screen."

Beneath the text lies a picture, presumably of their city, nestled between rolling green hills, a world away from BTS. Another user urges them to stay hopeful in the comment section, offering to give them hope if they need.

"I believe deep down that your love for them is strong," they write, "and that they will come to see you!!!"

Regardless of whether or not BTS perform in Columbia the user may never know them, even if they are to stand in the crowd at their idol's feet. Even if the idol is to reach down and touch them, they will never truly know one another. The user was right, the only way that they will be known to one another is through a screen.

There is no doubt that ARMY love BTS, but the ways in

Idol Limerence

which each individual loves the idol group, and in turn, the way the collective loves the group, is varied. Love for BTS is on a spectrum, each ARMY is passionate about BTS, each ARMY loves BTS; but what kind of love?

These expressions of love typically result in concentrated groupings of types of fans within the fandom. That is not to say that there is only one expression of love for one grouping of fans, rather there is a larger pattern that shows the link between what fans self-identify as to how they openly express their love and adoration for BTS.

On one end of the spectrum lies the majority; OT7, *One True 7*, who wish to celebrate BTS in their original form and whatever their next incarnations may be. They believe that each member is a vital part of the group, and wish for nothing more than for everyone to be happy in their pursuit of success, or whatever else it is they may be looking for. A lot of these fans love BTS members equally, but it is common for an ARMY to have a favourite which they refer to as a bias. There are also bias wreckers, meaning a member makes one question their allegiance to their original bias. These wreckers can be permanent favourites or on rotation dependent on small factors, they looked good during a music video; they looked at the audience a certain way during a live performance; they thrust their hips in such a way that the fan couldn't help but fall in love all over again.

Throughout all types of ARMY there are varying degrees of stans. Stan here does not refer to a man with the birth name of Stanley. Rather, stan is derived from an Eminem song of the same name wherein a, for lack of a better word, fan, kills himself and his wife over Eminem not replying to correspondence. In this context, stans are self titled as such for their above-normal levels of devotion to their group, idol or celebrity. There are soft stans, who want to braid their OT7's, biases or bias wrecker's hair and tuck them into bed, and there are hard stans. Who wants to play the same night time fantasy but with an f in the place of the t.

ARMY

Within this same area of the spectrum, comes those who *ship* particular members of the group. Or rather, one half of the *ship* category lies here; we'll call it the *friendship ship*, for lack of a better word. These are ARMY who love pairings of members, such as 2Seok (Seokjin and Hoseok) and share images of what they deem to be an endearing friendship. Their every action is analysed and theories are determined and spread throughout the internet. Their friendship is worshipped and praised with fan-made videos and photos; in a way the fans are celebrating the strong connection between band members. This still lies within the relatively neutral territory of the ARMY-loves-BTS-spectrum, though is nearing the middle. It's as if ARMY celebrate the friendship of BTS as if it were their own personal friendship with the group, an innocent act of vicarious living; a fantasy, an escape. Plus, who doesn't like to see healthy examples of complex, nuanced, high-stress male/male friendships?

Next to this lies the *relationship ship* category, where there are a number of fans dedicated to, what they believe to be, the genuine romantic relationship between members. The most evident of this is Vmin, the couple pairing of Taehyung and Jimin. Just like with the ship before, these shippers spend countless hours pouring over content to analyse the overt and subtle messages that lie within. They perpetuate the romantic love narrative of their favourites, for some it seems to be a playful past time, for others it's a serious undertaking. It's as if they love their idols so much they would rather see them with one another than anyone else, that is, if they can't be first in line themselves.

Now, if this were represented with a visual spectrum, there would be a large gap before the next category. Drag your eyes to the right of this page, keep going until you are no longer looking at the white, then go a little further. Perhaps turn your head a little to the side as you continue to drag your eyes further and further. Stop right before you feel like your neck may snap in two if you turn any further, we have reached our destination; solo stans. Solo stans are a different kettle of... the word fish comes to mind, but that would be unkind to our ocean dwelling friends. A solo stan has just one favourite member of a group, and they only want to see this one member succeed, even if it's at the expense of others. When ARMY are participating in global efforts to chart BTS' music, solo stans are often absent as they are boycotting the group. Their dream is to see the end of BTS so that their favourite can shine; they deeply believe that their bias is intentionally mistreated and held back by the group. It's not uncommon for solo stans to move in packs, working together to undermine the wider agenda of ARMY in the name of loving their idol. They believe to know their idol innately, better than anyone else in the world, swearing to not stop until their idol is crowned king above all else.

Lastly, further to the right comes a 사생, *sasaeng*, a fan who stalks their idol, believing that any attention is better than none. In a recent V Live titled *It's been forever, too,* Taehyung spoke about the group's decision to fly on private planes, saying that they wish they could fly commercially but whenever they do they are surrounded by sasaengs who have paid for information on their schedule and secured seats close to them. During another V Live, titled *BTS Live: After a Happy Time, a Relaxed Glass*, Jungkook receives a call from a sasaeng, which he says regularly happens. They presumably pay big money for access to the personal information of BTS. There have been recorded incidences of members of BTS being chased by sasaengs, which, when reading from the page might sound like regular fan activities; but are they really? To watch videos posted from sasaengs as they chase down their beloved idols is horrifying, members such as Taehyung go from peacefully walking through the airport to hearing the screams of two or three sasaengs, to walking faster, to running as people jump out of his way. A friend of Hoseok's sister was sent death threats and abused online after pictures surfaced of her posing with members of the group. Lastly, many sasaengs book rooms in the same hotels as BTS, and post pictures from inside implying that they are the romantic partner of a member. A rumpled bed, empty champagne glasses, a behind the scenes shot of an art gallery that Namjoon posted a picture from; these fabricated images are spread by the sasaengs to validate their narrative.

Not only is this a spectrum of love felt and shown towards BTS, it's a spectrum of idol limerence. When it comes to BTS, and similarly, other idol groups, all love experienced from fan to idol is limerence. It cannot be separate or other, as the context of the relationship is inherently single-sided, borne of a parasocial relationship which continues to be upheld and maintained by the idol group.

All feelings of love experienced and expressed towards BTS sit on an idol limerence scale, which speans from OT7 soft stans to sasaengs. Running parallel to this is the spectrum of emotion felt by ARMY, euphoric bliss at one end, between that and neutrality in the middle lies happiness, with the other end comprising of despair and suicide. Intersecting with these spectrums are meta themes of persona, shadow, reality and fantasy. Alongside these meta themes are other external factors that impact how the spectrums are experienced on individual and collective levels: sexuality, gender, socioeconomic status, geopolitical positioning, age, religion and race.

These spectrums and meta identity themes coexist within all of ARMY, plus far more; a complex phenomenon which cannot be examined in one book alone. Further, though they are displayed on a spectrum, that is not to say that these things can't be experienced in tandem, and not just linearly. For ARMY, these spectrums exist all at once, they come and go in waves, they give the fandom strength and, at the same time, drive them to all new lows.

The most evident expression of love towards BTS can be found no matter where one looks; it is the intersection of reality and euphoric happiness. It is the moment when the fan becomes one with ARMY and rejoices in an achievement of BTS; joyous celebration is by far the most commonly shared fan experience. When BTS announced their comeback during the first week of January, 2020 that defied the norms of K-pop, ARMY erupted in a chaotic outpouring of ecstatic love and elation. Firstly, it had been ten months since BTS' last comeback, the longest time between releases in their history; to say ARMY were excited was an understatement. Secondly, the enormity of such an ambitious comeback was almost too much for the fandom to fathom; it was so big that it needed a *comeback map* which showed a well plotted six-week course from the announcement to the release of *Map of the Soul: 7*. Ecstatic love as ARMY felt BTS had reciprocated their love to the power of seven, kind of like saying *ARMY, we love you this much^7*. Though many ARMY fantasise a scenario wherein they receive emotional reciprocation from BTS, there is nothing quite like living through a very real reciprocation in the form of an album release. Watching phenomenon, phenomena, in action, watching history unfold at the speed of a Twitter feed in meltdown and being able to actively participate in it; that is the root of joy for ARMY individually. This is made infinitely more sweet by the fact that it occurs in the collective. When ARMY become the collective they are no longer bound by their circumstance, it is just them and BTS standing eye to eye. An academic recently commented on BTS' most recent step in their comeback, Connect BTS which brings together 22 artists across multiple countries for a global exhibition of sorts. They said that BTS is creating an I-You-We with ARMY. However, this was never the case; it has always been I and Thou. I and Thou is the foundation of this global phenomenon, which has led to the existence of phenomena. ARMY celebrate when they and BTS each take equal part in acknowledging the cosmic love that flows between them; rejoicing in the universe relationally created in the infinite moments between here and now. The comeback map was not just plotting the well-laid plans to global domination; it was providing ARMY a map back home to stand with BTS. When we become I and Thou, when we experience a cosmic force of love so pure and strong, we do not just simply merge as one, rather we grow upwards together; through this we achieve a oneness.

Martin Heidegger, a German philosopher, in his book *Being and Time*, uses the word *dasein* which translates to *being-there*. According to Heidegger, *being* is for and with others, just like trees exist together as individuals in a collective. In that sense, ARMY and BTS are two tall trees in the same forest; between them is all of existence carried on a faint breeze. Euphoric, ecstatic love and elation doesn't begin to explain what ARMY feel when happiness and reality intersect on the spectrum simultaneously with millions around the world. Their feelings remain only truly known by BTS who stand opposite, watching on. Though they are tall trees rooted in reality, they reach towards the sky dreaming of a whole new world; they are *dasein*.

From here, experiences become more varied and hard to define in simple terms. Though there are infinite combinations of the spectrums and the many external factors that impact upon them, only a small number will be used as examples to demonstrate the complex individual experiences and expressions of love towards BTS.

An intersection of reality, soft stans, feelings of hope and a wishful fantasy can be found in another post on Weverse. A user shares an image that shows themselves and Jungkook posing before a mirror, they have edited themselves into the picture, showing their desire to be a part of Jungkook's life.

"My hobby right now is to fantasise and edit [photos] about them... where I fantasise as if it's a reality, I can only dream of meeting them, but I'm sure with my fantasies so far maybe it will probably come true some day. I believe it."

Fantasy becomes a hopeful reality upon the creation of an image that shows this user with their limerent focus, Jungkook. This post displays soft stan behaviour, their dream is to meet

Idol Limerence

BTS. As there is no mention of what else they might like to do with their idol, it remains up to the viewer to assume perhaps they dream of having a picnic and stargazing with Jungkook.

Perhaps the best example of limerent fantasies can be found within the realm of fan fiction, it exists on every person, group or topic imaginable. Limerence turns everyone into poets, artists, wordsmiths. The intersection of BTS and limerence makes for many long, descriptive sentences that slowly move the reader's eyes across the flawless faces of the idols. Tennov writes that limerent fantasies must be rooted in reality, and fan fiction shows exactly this; domestic bliss, the idol in private, the idol as man. Take this excerpt from a short story called *Stolen* by user *ponchowearingpinocchio* which revolves around a single scene of an early morning. The reader is placed in the position of the female who watches on while Jimin eats cereal in their, presumably shared, kitchen:

> As he collected the drops of milk with a small flick of his tongue, a small content smirk flashed across his face replacing them, dimples briefly pressed into the sides of his round cheeks. You watch the small rise and fall of his chest through the thin cotton t-shirt, eyes flickering to his neck, before returning your gaze to his beguiling, animated expression. His eyes shift to the next page, his head tilted just a little more to face you. It is like this that you examined him more carefully, taking time to linger over the small, wavy kinks in his light hair, noticing the way his lips curved when he smiled and how his cheeks coloured a deeper shade of crimson at this hour of the early morning.

Particular attention is paid to the smallest details of Jimin's hair, cheeks, lips, tongue and eyes; the story is written in such a way that the reader has no choice but to consume every aspect of a vulnerable Park Jimin as he reads a newspaper. He is constructed as wise and measured, someone who is usually bright and loud, but is warm and relaxed in this stolen morning; time plays a large part in this story. Soon he will be gone again, covered in sequins and full of untamed energy, but not today; today is for Jimin and [insert your name here].

ARMY

Most glaringly obvious of all; this book is in and of itself a prime example of idol limerence. Grounded in reality, it comprises social theory, philosophy, analytical psychology, cultural criticism and commentary. It takes the fixed timeline of BTS and mixes it with the fantasy, the fictitious life of Echo who is the physical embodiment of ARMY. It is both scholarly, to give credibility, and romantic to give an expression to oftentimes cringeworthy limerent musings. It heavily uses metaphors, heuristics to be more exact, relies heavily on subtext and, most of all; it harnesses limerence to create a whole new time and space for talking about the many phenomena present. Through this, the book argues for the existence of another realm of consciousness where the limerent can coexist face to face with the focus of their limerent desire. A fantasy that brings transient relief from the torturous, albeit welcomed, reality of being a high functioning sociologist with, what some would call, a cognitive disorder. Perhaps a new kind of superpower, being able to relate any theory, any event or feeling back to one idol in particular. Like limerence gives one seer-like abilities to see patterns otherwise invisible. This very book is the intersection of fantasy, reality, persona and shadow. The Echo narrative ranges from euphoria to suicidal and back again, it often isn't linear and errs on the side of relative immorality depending on how far one reads into the words left unspoken. The book attempts to hold both spectrums in their entirety and examine them. Further, through holding all the complexities, the book asks of Echo to experience as much as possible. The book takes Echo beyond the brink of her own sanity, and asks the same of the author. Life imitates art, the book is ARMY and BTS, the book is limerence; as is Echo who was borne of a creative neurosis. Echo perhaps can be understood as the shadow of a powerlifting sociologist who spent too much of their time trying to connect the dots. Just one lens, one possible reality, but not the only one.

The above are all manifestations of idol limerence, but one

Idol Limerence

thing needs to be made clear: idol limerence needn't be consciously known or acknowledged by the experiencer in order to exist. Love felt towards BTS will *always* uphold and perpetuate their dominance; whether the fan likes to say so or not. In a recent conversation with an ARMY familiar with the content of this book, the topic of limerence arose. His first thoughts were to differentiate his experience from the common experience of limerence, though his mind was provoked by the concept he felt that it didn't completely apply to him.

"I remind myself that I love them differently than some others might," he writes as he reflects through conversation, "the whole limerence idea makes total sense. I'm definitely a bit like that."

What he said next, however, is perhaps indicative of a greater trend within ARMY. He said that he, and his other friends who love BTS, realised he couldn't love them like *that*. Except *that* was emphasised as THAT. Which is to say, this ARMY felt he was limerent but felt he couldn't, or shouldn't be. For him, and for many other ARMY, Echo included, being seriously in love with BTS was a moral line they felt they couldn't cross. Interestingly, despite believing their feelings were immoral, not quite right, the feelings themselves prevail, and the narrative continues.

Most interestingly of all, many days after this conversation took place, this particular ARMY asked if limerence could be a force of good. If it was ok to be limerent. Which, of course, it is. Once learning this he was almost, no, completely relieved. The negative connotations attached to something that is often described as an offshoot of an obsessive compulsive disorder were so strong that he pushed his feelings aside, repressed them.

Somehow ARMY has managed to internalise the dominant discourse that serves to disempower people who experience the world differently, despite BTS' message being the polar opposite.

Perhaps, the repression of these limerent feelings leads to a particular kind of fan, which is seen in the extremes of the BTS-idol-limerence-spectrum. It could be argued that some repress their true feelings so much that they are converted into crude sexual fantasies that lack narrative or feeling; are manifested as aggressive solo stanning or, in extreme circumstances; look like becoming a sasaeng. Where desire and guilt are so intricately intertwined that they obscure the root of the issue; they want emotional reciprocation from their idols. Instead of, say, writing a book about it, they end up disrupting the democratic order of the fandom, and potentially endanger the lives of BTS and their loved ones. They become the ugly shadow borne of the complexity of an under-acknowledged limerence. However, shadows do not simply consist of things that are ugly; there is beauty in darkness, too.

Before it can be demonstrated in Chapter Seven that ARMY, like BTS, are revolutionaries, it must be first shown that BTS, like ARMY, can be perceived as being limerent, too.

"Hi everyone, my name is RM," Namjoon sits in his hotel room after a show in December, 2019, "I'm from South Korea, I'm 25."

He is speaking in English to demonstrate the low level of his voice. When he speaks Korean in interviews he changes how his voice sounds so that it's more easily understood. When he speaks casually to his friends his voice is much more similar to what it sounds like in English.

He pauses, tapping his hand on the table, trying to think of how he will conclude the example.

"I'm doing this V Live with my ARMYs, with my lovers."

Long before they debuted in June 2013, Namjoon, Seokjin, Yoongi, Hoseok, Jimin, Taehyung and Jungkook, as well as their team, consciously worked to turn seven individuals into BTS. First, BTS made themselves, second, they made an ARMY in their image; perhaps using their limerent imaginations. Then after that, after a critical mass of fans was accumulated, ARMY, presumably fuelled by limerence handed to them on a platter, an inheritance, of sorts, undertook the task of mirroring BTS. This freed up the idols to be visionaries in their own lives, knowing full well that an entire ARMY will follow suit. That is to say, BTS were the original limerents in this mutual romance narrative, and remain so to this very day. ARMY were simply created in the image of their idol and must live out a shadow life, of sorts, so that BTS may shine brighter against the contrast. It's hard to not become limerent when the content being delivered by the idol group can be interpreted as being, in and of itself, a limerent work of art. It's hard not to reflect limerence back when BTS use their platform to spread messages of love, self-love; romantic love; the kind of love that can shape and create universes; the kind of love that can change the world for the better.

Take their song *Heartbeat*, released June 2019, as an example. When it is examined through the lens of limerence, especially the way that idol limerence has been sociologically constructed in this book, a pattern begins to emerge. This is to say that Echo's experience, the experience of love, romance, limerence and idol limerence, is universal... or, as it's stylised in the music video for *Heartbeat*, youniversal, if you like.

Seems like I am locked deep in the dreamlike reality

Unrequited love, in this song, is constructed as the feeling of being seasick; existing in an altered state of reality, a dreamstate. Just like limerence, an unrequited love makes the experiencer feel like something isn't quite right, like they're stuck and unable to move without the person of their desire loving them back. Perhaps this dreamlike reality exists as the person in love is fantasising a scenario where their limerent focus confesses their love; where requited love provides a transient relief from the torment. Time moves differently in this reality, slower, faster, all at once, non-linear... and this person is locked, which implies that some of it is out of their control; they cannot exit this state until they hear an 'I love you, too'.

I know me before you was a ready-made me
But you designate me and you resume me

A ready-made 'me' could perhaps be interpreted as a persona

that was fabricated for a particular purpose, say, being an idol. This idol is now saying that when they met this person who they fell in love with, they were remade, reborn. This unrequited love made them deconstruct their past persona and reconstruct anew. Through the use of the dreamlike state the person in love, the idol, can use their imagination to see how the focus of their desire would view them, it's here that limerence can lead to the deconstruction of a ready-made persona. Persona and limerence are the only two that can deconstruct and reconstruct one another; people in unrequited love engage in this radical transformation regularly, shapeshifting to best suit their one and only.

Been calling your name in this whole universe
Now I need no space, I got youniverse

Limerence is a yearning for another, a longing, a never-ending search for the other half so that one can become whole. Sometimes limerence is just a longing for love itself, other times limerence is a yearning for the love of a particular someone who, perhaps, doesn't yet know your name. When this person is located, when the focus of a limerent desire is found, the limerence intensifies. It is here, in the dreamlike state, in a fantasy realm, that the limerent and their desire can first meet. It is here, when they stand eye to eye that the universe exists between them; all of existence as we know it is relational. That is to say, it does not exist outside of You and I; two equals. Everything, every tiny little thing, exists in the space between limerent and focus. Buber says that love is a cosmic force, and limerence says that this cosmic love exists between I and Thou. There's no need for space, or time, when I've got Youniverse.

I feel the destiny in you you you you you
Feel the destiny in me me me me me

Lastly, limerence brings with it the feeling that this special kind of love is predestined. All the collective unconscious moves to bring people together who recognise the same patterns, who hear the same sounds, who interpret the archetypes the same

Idol Limerence

way; this is how the unconscious learns and grows. Just like the universe existing between I and You, the collective unconscious exists relationally. This feeling of destiny exists to call us home, propels us forward, brings new people into our lives so that we may ascend to new levels of consciousness and perhaps become revolutionaries in a brave new world. This sense of familiarity cannot be shaken, for it dates back to the start of time. These archetypes, these symbols and feelings and words are so deeply embedded in the evolution of humankind that it is simply not possible to ignore; love is destiny. Limerence is an extreme manifestation that exists to pull us together against all odds, calling us back to our soul purpose: to love one another.

It could be argued that when BTS originally thought about who they each wanted to be as idols, and collectively as a group, that they harnessed this state of limerence to construct themselves in many different scenarios. Limerence in the sense that they had a yearning for something, a longing to belong and to have their voices heard. A love for music, a love for dance, a love for performing. Idol limerence isn't limited to existing human-to-human, it can be human-to-idea, human-to-feeling. Through limerence they would have entered into a dreamstate, a fantasy, where they could construct themselves any way they pleased. It is also here that they could use their imaginations to see themselves in the eyes of others. Others, presumably, such as their future fans. Long before ARMY fell in love with BTS, BTS fell in love with an idea, a feeling, of who or what they wanted to be in the future. It was this love, this passion, this limerence that drove them forward; nothing else creates such a force of energy quite like limerence. Limerence is creational energy, universal energy, cosmic energy. There is no other energy quite like limerence, and at one point or another, BTS presumably used it in the construction of their carefully made personas.

Once they had constructed themselves, envisaged who they wanted to be as idols and as a group, BTS, presumably, set out to imagine what their fan base could be like. Who would listen to their music? Who would buy their merch? Who would share their photos online? Who would pay to see them perform? These are questions any musician, any creative surely would ask of themselves. It is here that BTS starts to shape who ARMY are, for in many ways their fan base would be a reflection of them. A fan base that likes the same music as BTS, a fan base that resonates with the message BTS communicates, a fan base that finds the idol personas not only relatable, but attractive and desirable. BTS were their own fans first, having to fall in love with an idea of who they could be if all their wildest dreams come true. They then fostered these fans in their image; who better to base a desirable fan on but the idol themselves? This process can be the origin story of idol limerence, if you like, though idol limerence is just one lens to use, one of many; it's rose-coloured at best.

Interestingly, through this process, built on love, ARMY can become the ideal muse for BTS. On one hand, the group wants to give back to their dedicated fan base, so they write with ARMY in mind; perhaps they harness their limerent imaginations to think of how ARMY would perceive certain lyrics or visuals. On the other, ARMY could take on the form of anyone in the minds of the idols; they could look like one person, they could shapeshift to suit whatever scenario is required in a creative process. An endless source of inspiration is provided by the millions of adoring fans. What is to stop an idol turning their mind to those who love them most, their fans, when stuck writing a love song?

So when Namjoon says that ARMY are his lovers, it makes sense. There is an exchange of love between ARMY and Namjoon, and BTS. For the period of time Namjoon is an idol, his heart is to lie with ARMY who inspires and uplift him, just as he does in return. Perhaps most interestingly of all, in this make-believe scenario which Namjoon constructs to demonstrate his voice when speaking English, he introduces himself as RM; as

175

idol. He does not state that he, as Namjoon, is with his ARMYs, his lovers. Rather, his persona RM is the one who has millions of lovers, it is RM who is emotionally intimate with his fans. It is RM who is the interface between Namjoon, the human, and ARMY, the limerents. It is RM with the heart big enough to hold an entire universe of lovers, of love, and all the complexities that come with it, not Namjoon. And yet it still remains to be Namjoon, consciously using his persona as a reflexive tool for change and love. A persona that, to some degree, protects him and enables him to remain revolutionary, visionary, while RM holds all of existence in the space between idol and fan.

When BTS release a song that can be perceived as being inherently limerent, which is consumed by people who are, presumably, limerent themselves, the limerence grows in strength, in intensity. You see, limerence causes the limerent to be hyper-aware of everything their desire produces, creates. They are already reading into every subtlety and connecting the dots that perhaps do not even exist. They will relate everything back to a mutual romance narrative that they formulate in their minds, no matter how illogical. So when the limerent focus is limerent themselves, saying things like "feel the destiny in me", the limerence grows tenfold. It affirms the belief that their love is destined, even if the idol is singing about something entirely unrelated. Although, in this case, they are still singing about a form of limerence, an unrequited love, but towards whom it is unclear. So the limerent does what a limerent does best, they become a detective of the ways of their idol's heart, inevitably linking all thoughts back to the one truth they wish to pull forth from the dream realm into reality: their idol loves them back.

It can be argued that BTS created ARMY in their image with the use of limerence, that ARMY deconstruct and reconstruct themselves to better align with their idols; to be better versions of themselves to be more desirable. But that is not where it ends, this is just where it begins. ARMY are the mirror image of BTS, but instead of being one mirror it's more like a room of mirrors in which BTS stand; an infinite reflection that eventually becomes warped beyond recognition stretches out before them, behind them, above them. Their reflection surrounds them entirely and spans a universe. ARMY exist in the space between BTS members; they are one and the same.

If BTS are persona, then ARMY must be shadow. Though ARMY are powerful, they can often be toxic towards one another and the world around them. There are many negative manifestations of limerence that exist within ARMY, some so extreme that they seek to hurt members of BTS, their company and their loved ones. This is one side of a shadow, most definitely, but it is not the only one.

Shadow can be anything hidden, hidden because it has been deemed less desirable, perhaps an element that does not perfectly fit with the carefully constructed persona. It could be empathy, it could be a penchant for painting flowers on sidewalks, it could be a love for knowledge; it needn't be inherently bad to be found within the shadow realms. Moving away from a purely Jungian view of shadow, ARMY are the manifestation of all that BTS cannot be. In many ways, ARMY can live the lives that BTS can never experience, and vice versa. ARMY have more privacy, different levels of autonomy, different responsibilities, a better sleep schedule, visible tattoos; ARMY needn't censor nor hide parts of themselves in the same way BTS does. In a way, as ARMY can live vicariously through BTS, BTS can do the same with their fans. When they close their eyes they can lead a life of charmed mediocrity, they can hold hands with whoever they please and walk down a busy city street, they can remain anonymous in a crowded room.

To use an earlier metaphor adapted from *Whalien 52*, BTS as idols must be drowning on the world stage to maintain the public's interest in them. That is to say, they must knowingly change and torture themselves, adapt to a new way of being, in order to live as an idol who is both subject and object, powerful and powerless. They drown and we clap, wide eyed and full of awe at the superhuman feat of a life lived so vibrantly right before our very eyes. So, if the idol is voluntarily drowning, who is standing ashore breathing in their place? ARMY, of course. Connected through limerence, the fantasy state that takes them to this new world where they exist with BTS, the fan is able to breathe in their place in the here and now. Fuelled by a reciprocated love in another realm. Or, as Namjoon said in a 2018 interview with Dispatch Magazine, "through our music, through our stages, we are breathing together". Teamwork makes the dream work, after all.

There is beauty in darkness, BTS shows this time again with their haunting self-reflections in lyrics spread far across their discography. This darkness is personified, amplified in the millions of ARMY who take these messages to heart and transform them, first into an act of personal reflection and change, then from there, social change. ARMY are the shadow to BTS' persona, the other side of the idol coin; a powerful binary in which the universe exists between. Echo just hadn't seen it yet, she had only seen the bad which she feared lived within her repressed shadow self; she was afraid that by being limerent she would ultimately hurt Namjoon.

The train was close now, Echo could feel the heat from the lights on her face.

She thought of the time RM stood with her in the room with her many selves and remembered the version of her she couldn't quite look at.

She realised now, as she faced her other self in her memory, staring into her own eyes, that she had a shadow that she had to accept.

RM knew a lot of things that day that he didn't tell her, and this was one of them. Within her shadow self lay her darkest secrets, everything she submerged, out of view of her persona;

ARMY

out of view of Namjoon. It was the darkest aspects of ARMY, their shadow, that she saw within herself. When she refused to be an ARMY she was merely reacting to the fact that she was scared, scared of becoming *one of them*. When she wrote the monologue she delved even deeper into that fear until she became one, a sasaeng. Conflicted by her exploration of a relationship with Namjoon so much that she nearly split in two; Echo felt she didn't know herself anymore. How was she meant to feel? What was wrong and what was right? She was so scared of crossing the bounds of morality that she couldn't move from the train tracks. She had channeled all of ARMY but couldn't see any of their positive traits, it's as if they all passed through her and left their shadows imprinted on the backs of her eyelids. She wanted Namjoon to love her, but knew he could not. At least, not in the way she wished for. But no matter how hard she tried to ignore the limerence it wouldn't go away; her shadows wouldn't leave. Her torment, never ending.

As her life flashed before her eyes Echo couldn't help but gasp. She had a revelation.

The world crashed back down around her as she crawled backwards off the tracks.

The train blew past, an inch from her nose.

"I am ARMY."

RM sat on the opposite side of the train as it sped past, his eyes barely visible through the gaps in the carriages.

"All of ARMY is within me?"

RM bowed his head slightly.

"We are the same, ARMY and I, I get that now," Echo called out to RM.

She paused, the train no longer between them as they stood either side of the tracks in the dead of night.

"We are one."

RM smiled.

We are one, he replied.

Revolutionary

We are together bulletproof
—We Are Bulletproof: The Eternal, BTS

Remember, remember, the 5th of November. In 2032 the United Kingdom is ruled by Nordfire, a Nordist and neo-facist political party. A vigilante named V, face covered with a Guy Fawkes mask, blows up the Old Bailey. He then takes to television screens to urge everyone to rise against the government with him in a years time on Guy Fawkes night, November 5. Earlier that day he had rescued Evey, a young reporter, from members of the secret police. He takes her to his home and tells her to stay with him for the year leading up to his planned revolution. Evey escapes, only to be later captured by the government and tortured for the whereabouts of V. She is given an ultimatum, reveal V's location or be executed; she says she would rather die. At this point she is released, and soon discovers that she had been held at V's house all along; he was the one who had been torturing her. Though she is angry at first, she grows to love V, knowing he has made her stronger. It's soon November 5 and thousands of citizens march towards the House of Parliament wearing Guy Fawkes masks. Parliament is destroyed, the government overthrown by anarchy and people-power. When asked

Revolutionary

who V really was, Evey responds 'he was all of us.' *V for Vendetta* demonstrates a revolution typically seen throughout history, riddled with violence and misery. V shows us that in any good revolution, the power lies in the masses; with the people who reflect the revolutionary themselves.

It's May 11 2018, Namjoon records himself talking about preparations for BTS' comeback; it's an RM vlog reminiscent of those posted pre-debut. The vlog isn't posted until March 2019, two days after the release of the *Persona* music video. Timing is everything, and in this instance could hardly be seen as a mistake. Maybe, just maybe, the intention expressed in the 2018 vlog came into fruition in March 2019. Maybe, just maybe, Big Hit wanted to demonstrate the foresight, the vision, of Namjoon to illustrate a much larger picture that encompasses more than just an album release. Rather, it encompasses an entire revolution; a well-laid plan that started long before BTS formed. A plan that now took on new life and was carried on the message of one man, Namjoon, and became the message of an entire group, BTS.

'As ever, I won't forget that when I speak I'm doing so as the spokesperson of the group, I will proceed in that manner. The role that I can undertake now is to view everything more positively.'

'They say you can change the world in exactly two ways: first, to become a revolutionary, second, to view the world positively. I want to do both, I'm going to succeed at both.'

Historically there have been numerous revolutions, usually started as acts of rebellion against regimes. Revolutions, more often than not, begin as a power-grab and go on to influence how money gets made, which over the course of time has looked like revolutions of the agricultural industry. In contemporary times it is not all about food, though vegans who are charged as eco-terrorists in Australia would beg to differ. Rather, modern-day revolutions revolve around politics, government structures and the alluring power of controlling armed forces. Marx predicted a revolution of sorts, where the working class would rise up against the ruling elite and overthrow them. However, his very words were used to create a different kind of revolution that stood in stark opposition to his vision; communism and dictatorships, for Marx, were never meant to mix. Which shows that an idea can start a revolution, but not always the right one. A revolution is more than just an idea, which is why Marx cannot be seen as a true revolutionary; he wasn't ever around to see his concept of communism through to the end. He wrote, he theorised, but he never put words into action; he was not a leader.

History hasn't shown a revolutionary quite like Namjoon, nor BTS, as all history can show is hurt men hurting men in an attempt at possessing an elusive power and ruling with brute force. When it comes to the Namjoon narrative, the first step to becoming a revolutionary is to change the meaning of the word itself, or rather, change the mode and means of which a revolution begins and, ultimately, how it ends. This isn't a hostile takeover, this is a revolution of consciousness; the coming of the Age of Aquarius which many have hoped to be a return to love for humankind. If history has shown us that hurt men hurt men, BTS shows us that loved men loving men is far more powerful; a power which can only be attained when it is not sought after nor even thought of in the first place.

Who better than to lead this revolution than the man who wrote "I live so I love", and who better to be right by his side than those he loves most. Those who are a map to his insides, the map of his soul; the one true 7 that, only when together, become whole.

A revolutionary in the 21st century must surely be a physical embodiment of love, love in every sense of the word. Love from the inside out, love that extends from deep within all the way up to the stars in the sky and out into the vast universe beyond.

Revolutionary

Someone who understands the transformational power of love, someone who has first started to love themselves. The same someone who basks in the healing light of a revolutionary love from their many selves reflected back at them amidst a sea of purple orbs. Someone who knows that love isn't easy, and the biggest battle lies within; it starts and ends with a revolution of the self.

The most controversial, rebellious act any one person can do is to love themselves, to continue to recommit to the process through the ups and downs of a life that isn't designed to allow one to become self-actualised. This love isn't perfect or complete, it's a love that is a perpetual work in progress as reality shifts around it. It's a love that transcends and is so big that it can elevate millions, billions, to brave new heights.

In a world that burns and drowns; while melting and freezing; where the rich get richer and the poor are downtrodden and dying; where the animals scream for help before making it to our dinner plates while we remain distracted, transfixed by a hurt man with his finger hovering over a button called WW3... who is it that is coming to help? We spend our nights watching superheroes save our world over and over, yet we know that it's not Superman who will save us, that's what makes superheroes so good. It's a reality we will never truly know, yet desperately need.

It's not an alien with laser vision that is our saviour, in fact, the answers to saving the world have been within us all along; we have to be our own superhero. But we are disenchanted, we are hurt and we are dying, what we really need is for someone to lead the way and we will gladly follow. In a world of hurt men hurting men, it cannot be just women who stand against them, that will only perpetuate the dangerous, lethal binary that sees the biggest threat to a woman in the West, and everywhere else, an angry white man. Change must first come from a man with love, or rather, a *Boy With Luv*, to other men which will open space for women, and those who lay elsewhere on the gender spectrum, to stand as equals; as revolutionaries.

Traditionally, it has been the leader of an army who stands triumphant at the end of a rebellion; this time the only difference is not just capitalism, but capitalisation. The largest army on Earth has 1.6 million troops armed with guns, they'll shoot to kill. BTS' ARMY, however, is estimated to be 23 million strong, armed with lightsticks called *bombs*, they shoot love hearts from finger guns; their motto is *click-click, bang bang, we are bulletproof*. There needn't be a dictatorship to recruit members to this army, in fact, they'll pay for the privilege; this revolution has reappropriated the words army, bomb and bulletproof to stand for love, acceptance and nonviolence. How ironic, then, that the one thing that could tear BTS and ARMY apart may be South Korea's mandatory military enlistment, 2020 might just be the last time we see OT7 for quite some time.

So if the leader of a rebellion, a revolution, is also the leader of an almighty army, then it is Namjoon who is the revolutionary of our times. It is a man with love, who is love, who has a reflexive persona that allows him to be a conduit of love for millions; this revolutionary is a man split in two, who is drowning so that we may breathe. He is writer, he is artist, he is musician, he is persona, he is idol, he is leader, he is love, he is revolutionary; most importantly of all, he is human who is just a reflection of us all. If he can be a revolutionary, that means we can be one, too.

This revolution started where any great revolution should; a revolution of the self. If a revolution, in the context of this book, is to be rooted in love, then a revolution of the self can only mean one thing: love yourself. This in and of itself changes the world, even if it begins with expressing an intention to try and love oneself and doesn't quite make it to the next step straight away. Understanding that self-love should be one's first priority is a revolutionary act, but it is the process of self-love that is the true battle. In a sense it is won before it even begins, as a choice to move towards self-love is an act of self-love in itself. However, if self-love is a battle it must be fought on two fronts: a battle of the competing selves, and a battle of the world vs. self. Self-love is a never-ending process, it is a muscle that must be grown and maintained over time, just like the heart is a muscle; we must use it in order for it to continue working.

So if a revolution, and in turn, a revolutionary, begins with the process of self-love, why is it that Kim Namjoon, and BTS, are singled out as the forefront of this movement? Self-love is often a process kept behind closed doors, relegated to the realms of airy self-improvement movements that are dismissed as soft, and therefore pointless. The two concepts of self and of love are often associated with more effeminate people; self-love is for women, and therefore pointless, as men simply do not have feelings, nor need they love themselves. This discourse exists purely to perpetuate our own emotional and spiritual disempowerment, a discourse which is rapidly shifting beneath our feet.

When embarking on this journey of self-love, BTS as a group of men began a discourse of learning to love themselves that extended further than their own private quarters. Not only that, they didn't merely say it in passing or make a simple Tweet; they made a trilogy on it. You see, a revolutionary must be an artist, must be a musician for many reasons. In this case, it is the transcendent properties of music that reach beyond language and culture; it is music that follows us wherever we go, not words on a page in an odd-looking book. Music finds us anywhere, any time, and communicates complexities in simple terms that retain their nuances, especially when the Korean language is involved.

Suddenly, the words *love yourself* take on new meaning, they are no longer words one would find in a small corner of a darkened bookstore. They are art, with many implicit and explicit meanings now attached as BTS use them to further their individual and collective narrative, both fictional and reflective. They are commodity, packaged in aesthetically pleasing ways that delight the heart and mind; a gift which we gladly pay for. But most of all, they are words that come from the mouths of men who sit with one another and reflect on their lives, their shared journey and struggles, while the camera records and the world watches on. Suddenly, self-love is a word, a concept, for everyone; even men, even idols. Suddenly, the idea of loving oneself is accessible to anyone as the stigma begins to shift. Then comes the magic, watching self-love in progress from a group of seven men with the weight of the world on their shoulders. That's why it must come from artists, musicians, in fact, that is why it must come from an idol; no one enraptures the world quite like a seemingly perfect idol. Who better to teach a new generation of people to love themselves than an idol who proclaims they are inherently flawed and spend most of their time hating themselves? After all, what we love about idols is that they're just like us; not many of us love the skin we're in. But that is changing as we shape ourselves in the reflection of our beloved idols, our limerent desires, who show us how personas can be made and remade; this time our persona is love, made in their image.

Similar to how this book is set out, the *Love Yourself* trilogy had three distinct parts, which came in the form of two mini albums and a studio album. *Love Yourself: Her* came first and represented the development phase of the series; it explored the many different experiences of interpersonal love, much like the beginning of this book. Next came *Love Yourself: Tear* which represented the turn, the twist if you like, which highlights the darker, sadder aspects of love; much like the middle of this book. Lastly came *Love Yourself: Answer*, the conclusion, which within it held the answers, a way forward. The answer, of course, was that one must first love themselves. But what exactly was the question? Perhaps what this trilogy demonstrated was a universally understood journey to find love with another, something which we all desire. A journey which ended with finding a far better love; a love from within which ultimately allows one to give and receive far more love than ever before.

This revolution started with a revolution of the self, a commitment between friends to love themselves more, better than

Revolutionary

before. This moved from the personal to the interpersonal to societal as it extended to a movement amongst ARMY who sought to love themselves better, at the request of their idols. Through this, the act of self-love became political defiance of societal norms which seek to separate and segregate us through socially constructed means; countries, borders, language, culture, religion, identity, gender, sexuality, time and place. Self-love no longer became a lonely journey, it was a mutual, ongoing journey that still exists to this day and continues to be a theme throughout the work and message of BTS. This is reflected through the simultaneous process which ARMY embark on, day in and day out, as they discover and rediscover songs, videos, interviews, and find comfort in sharing their journey on and offline with others. In this nonlinear process there is one thing that holds it all together; community, ARMY, and through them: love.

Which brings about the second step in the Kim Namjoon, BTS, revolutionary narrative; revolutions are best shared with friends. What better friends exist than those within BTS? A self-love turned outwards is a love for friends amidst adversity, struggle and ultimately, triumph. But most importantly, this is a love shared between male friends which has shown the world how men can be loving towards one another. Not just any men, men who work and live together, men who are idols. Why is it that millions of people watch videos of BTS sitting around a table reflecting on another year gone? What is it that makes a glimpse behind the scenes of preparations for a tour so enthralling? It's the process, it's watching seven men deal with complexities together while holding hands, sharing beds, crying in a dressing room and wishing they could have done better. Watching how these artists, idols, are genuinely humble amidst the chaos.

The crowd is chanting their names, louder and louder, but they are not prancing around like show ponies, as one might expect. Rather, they are telling themselves they have to do better, give more energy despite having nothing left to give. They are giving and receiving feedback while tensions run high. They are listening and being heard, even if they are not being agreed with. They are expressing their innermost thoughts and feelings to one another, right there on the spot, committed to honesty and humility; committed to the process.

This is not what the West is used to seeing from musicians, a level of reflection and love in action between men at the top of their game. On the voiceover for their docuseries, *Bring the Soul*, all they say is "I am happy in this moment", and ask "How do we do better?" They are unafraid to show the pressure they are under, yet they do not display it in a way that demands sympathy, rather it provides an avenue for greater empathy. It's measured, thoughtful, it shows the true cost of a life of an idol; the loneliness, the lack of connection to the outside world, the extreme pressure of singing and dancing night after night while flying across the world.

How interesting that, from the outside looking in, the idol is leading a life of luxury. But from the inside looking out, they are in a windowless room trying to sleep on tiny couches before soundchecking, getting ready and performing to tens of thousands of people, which they do again and again, until it's done. None of it is easy, but what carries them through the ups and downs of a tour, of life as an idol, is the process.

Even though the viewer may not be an idol, perhaps not even an artist, watching seven young men negotiate the complexity of their situation provides countless life lessons. This is how men love other men, love isn't passive, nor is it easy. Love can mean telling someone they're wrong, love can look like a lot of listening even when you don't want to, love can look like two men holding hands; BTS are normalising platonic affection between men in the public eye.

What all of this means is that, if they are indeed revolutionaries, those who walk with them, ARMY, who are created in their image, perpetuate the same loving processes. Not only self-love, but an affectionate love for others that is not passive; it's a love through adversity and triumph. It's an unconditional love, unlike anything the world has seen before. This kind of love is, once again, an act of defiance; especially as it's between men. This is a love that heals, not only the members within BTS, but all those who look on. It changes perceptions of what male-male love need be, it normalises the act of men sharing a bed, men cuddling on a couch, men stroking one another's hair. All these acts are normalised in childhood between friends, but somewhere along the way the prejudice and fear sets in and we tear our children apart, we tell them it's not ok to touch anymore. We isolate them physically, then emotionally, then socially. Which makes up one small part of why men are hurt, which feeds into why men hurt women and other men; it all starts in one's childhood.

Yet watching Jimin and Taehyung hold hands at the airport is oddly healing, it gives a spark of energy and life. It tells the world 'I love my friend and that's ok', and over time the world adjusts to this, as it becomes a normal fact of life.

It is equally healing when Namjoon and Taehyung share a bed during season four of *Bon Voyage*, where BTS are in New Zealand, sleeping split between a campervan and tent.

"Can I hold you while I sleep?" asks Taehyung softly.

"That's going too far. Let's respect the distance between us," Namjoon replies.

"You do like me, right?" Taehyung asks.

"Of course. But that's different from sleeping in each other's arms."

"Why? What's wrong with holding each other?"

A pause.

"Can I hold your hand, at least?"

Just like that, it was demonstrated to the world how to ask permission for intimacy. An intimacy between men which was normalised by the simple act of including the scene in the episode; they could have cut it. Instead it was an endearing moment between friends, where one wanted to cuddle and the other didn't. Healing on two fronts: a man asking another for intimacy heals those who have been made to feel guilty, different, other, for wanting such a thing; a man asking for permission shows us all, especially women, that men can, in fact, ask before touching. Further, they can take a no without their world ending, they can be told no and respect a boundary; showing people everywhere what acceptable male behaviour looks like. No means no, yes means yes: BTS edition.

Friendship was the foundation on which BTS was built, and it's this friendship that makes them so alluring as a group. They are young men who are creators, visionaries, artists, but their talent wouldn't mean as much if it weren't evident that they were deeply in love with, and committed to, one another. There's something magical about friendship, especially the kind that can change the world. It wouldn't be a revolution without the friendship, the love, that BTS share between themselves. As Buber says, love is a cosmic force, and the universe only exists relationally; so existence is between each member, it is between each member that ARMY lives and breathes. It's complicated, but also, it's not; we are all one and nothing exists outside of us as we know *us* to be.

Do the stars really exist up in the sky if we do not have a mind that can comprehend them? Do we not look to the stars and experience them as humans, in relation to other humans, wishing we had someone to share that moment with? None of us have seen the stars up close, touched them with our hands and yet we know they exist for we are told they exist; so they do, because we make them. It is us as humans, with our words and our minds and our hands and our mouths and our eyes that give meaning to everything, meaning that only matters, only becomes real when it's shared.

After a revolution of the self is shared with friends, it must

Revolutionary

next be shared with a community. Knowledge is power, historically reserved for the wealthy elite, but a true revolutionary does not hoard their knowledge. In the BTS revolution each member of their ARMY must be equipped with the same set of skills as their talented leaders. Instead of asserting dominance through an intellectual imperialism, BTS freely share their experiences and upskill their followers. They do so that ARMY may continue to carry the message of this love revolution with more power and meaning than seven people could ever wield.

It only becomes a revolution when the masses become involved, and ARMY have been a part of this revolution from the start. In fact, they are co-creators of the revolution in more ways than one; another revolutionary act in itself. The idol and fan stand as relative equals. That is to say, as much as equals can exist within a binary, as one still holds and exerts power over the other to some degree. Both BTS and ARMY actively create and maintain each other's personas and more. Notably, a feat which could not occur without limerence, but more on that later.

Much like how life is only real when it is shared, knowledge is only knowledge when it is freely accessible to the masses. Anything else that comes with a price tag is merely a capitalist ruse, created so that the wealthy elite can feel as if they have something inside their minds that is good and pure. What they're buying is just an illusion of knowledge, real knowledge exists within the collective and holds no price tag and needs no thesaurus. Though it could be argued that BTS are now among the wealthy elite, they are by no means hoarding their knowledge for fear of others stumbling upon it and putting it to good use.

You see, what the 1% do not understand is that knowledge is also like money, it multiplies when shared. Rather, they do know it, but they are insecure, afraid they will no longer be needed nor relevant without their wads of cash and private jets that melt ice caps. This metaphor isn't about trickle down economics, it's more Keynesian than not; give money to the masses and they will stimulate the economy. Take money from the masses, leave them impoverished and malaised, and the economy will inevitably crash. The same applies to knowledge, and it is true that knowledge is power, which is why they, the ruling class, do not wish for us to have it. For when we realise that if we simply stand together and demand change, we will truly be unstoppable, just like the BTS lyric suggests: *we are together bulletproof.*

That's what scares the ruling elite, the global collective waking up to how they are continually dominated and controlled. But that does not scare BTS, for they are artists, and the world may burn and eat the rich; but art will live on forever. The ruling elite are hungry for power, which is why they will never truly have it. BTS are hungry for change, which is why they currently hold the power whether the West acknowledges it or not; it can only be truly possessed when it is not sought after. It can only truly be given, not demanded or taken.

What gives BTS power is ARMY, and the giving goes both ways. A revolutionary unsettles the power dynamic; idol and fan are now co-conspirators, to a certain degree, both giving and holding power freely, willingly. As much as anyone under capitalism can do anything freely or willingly, that is.

BTS, first and foremost, have always been about young people, as they started as young people and still are young men. In their earlier works they were highly political, covering topics such as classism and capitalism. They focussed on the education system in particular, highlighting the unfair societal expectations of young people. Though, it can be seen and argued, that their lyrics and message have always contained a reflective element, their work grew to become more introspective over time. This has been seen by many critics as a divergence from a stronger political analysis towards something more crowd-pleasing. However, it could be counter-argued that BTS remain as political as ever, now focusing on the politics of identity, the highly politicised nature of the self. Interestingly, new music doesn't cancel out the existence of the old, and as they continue to grow they bring with them the breadth of their earlier, drastically underrated

Revolutionary

works. The benefit of hindsight, they are connecting their work into a full loop. They have brought back samples of earlier songs in new releases, such as *Intro: Skool Luv Affair* from 2014 appearing in *Intro: Persona* released 2019, *Intro: O!RUL8,2?* from 2013 in *Interlude: Shadow* released January 2020 and *Intro: 2 Cool 4 Skool* from 2013 in *Outro: Ego* released February 2020. This demonstrates BTS' mindful acknowledgement that their work all sits as part of the same story, and it all remains relevant.

A new wave of criticism has headed for BTS this year, 2020, as they delve deeper into the map of their soul, continuing on a Jungian analysis of self started with *Map of the Soul: Persona* in 2019. What BTS are doing in the lead up to their next album, *Map of the Soul: 7*, has solidified them as highly contentious revolutionaries of the art world.

Connect, BTS is a global art project connecting five cities and twenty two artists who share a similar philosophy to BTS. The aim of the project, as written on the *Connect, BTS* website is to "redefine the relationships between art and music, the material and immaterial, artists and their audiences, artists and artists, theory and practice." Most interestingly of all, this entire project has been funded out of the pockets of BTS themselves; it's their gift to ARMY. So why is it that such an ambitious and globally significant art project is being met with disdain?

In an article published on *Hello Asia* titled *BTS Are The World's Most Revolutionary Artists Right Now: Here's Why It's Making People Uncomfortable*, authors Anastasia Giggins, Wallea Eaglehawk and K-Ci Williams analyse the response to *Connect, BTS*. The article argues that perhaps the cynicism towards the art project is symptomatic of a long-held xenophobia, except in the subtext there is no "perhaps". A xenophobia which has now manifested "as a distaste for BTS, worn like a badge of honour by intellectual imperialists with a large enough platform to grant them a verified opinion." You see, the arguments formed against the significance of *Connect, BTS* boil down to two main statements: the first is that we shouldn't take the project seriously as it comes from a pop group; the second is that it must be for publicity, therefore disingenuous, therefore not art.

As the article goes on to argue, it's "as if, somehow, pop isn't music, or if pop is music then there is no intersection between music and art." It's as if these critics are arguing music isn't art, but we all know that not to be true. So what exactly is the problem with musicians funding art? Perhaps, it comes down to how the idol is perceived, the Korean idol to be exact. You see, BTS, especially through this project, are showing themselves to be both subject and object; the complex binary previously explored in the earlier part of this book. Complex also in the sense that the West doesn't know how to consume something that is also a someone. Cows are beef, sheep are mutton; it's easier to eat something when you don't think about its face. The same goes with the idol, they're easier to eat whole right up until the mask comes off and one is eye-to-eye with the person beneath. When the West doesn't quite know how to classify something in order to unhinge their jaw and swallow they simply reject it; relegating it to the 'too hard' pile, claiming it to be the infantile interest of a mindless youth.

But here's the real catch; the youth aren't mindless. Especially not when art, previously reserved for the wealthy, becomes readily available, free to the public courtesy of BTS. Stephanie Rosenthal, director of Berlin's Gropius Bau, said they cannot usually afford to offer free public programming. Yet, thanks to BTS, they were able to open their doors to everyone between January 15 and February 2 for *Rituals of Care*, a performance series which offered "radical acts of care" through "a range of sonic techniques, queer re-imaginings and indigenous perspectives". A new generation of people were able to access not only art at a famous cultural institution, but they were able to receive radical healing. No wonder people are uncomfortable, BTS aren't just making a simple gallery tour free, they're giving a pla-

Revolutionary

tform to contemporary, political, controversial works that heal and empower not just a few; but potentially the entire world.

It is through initiatives such as *Connect, BTS* that we can begin to see how BTS are changing their own industry; which, in the revolutionary trajectory, is the next step. First was a revolution of the self; second was a revolution shared with friends, and; third came a revolution of a community. Here, at the intersection of community and industry, and further, at the intersection of art, community and industry, we find BTS' use of the *network-image*.

Film and Deleuzian philosopher 이지영 Lee Jiyoung proposes the new concept of *network-image* in her book *BTS, Art Revolution*. Lee describes the "cross-referential open structure" of BTS' music videos which refer to other online content and albums, as well as content and albums from the past, and the future. Lee writes that this particular nature of the videos can only be actualised through the active participation of the spectator, the fan. Through this they become a part of the BTS universe, the narrative, as active members in the journey. They become a part of the production of the art, and their involvement can change the very nature of the art itself. According to Lee, "the BTS phenomenon points to a shift in the total nature of art", which calls for a new concept, the network-image. This art does not pursue truth, contemplation or the beauty of supremacy. Rather, the social role is sharing value, the generation of meaning through sharing which grows and changes as it spreads throughout the network. Lee writes that the network-image being shared and created between BTS and ARMY is a new art form, "an instance of a beautiful encounter between politics and aesthetics."

This intersection of art, in the form of a music video, meets community when it's shared with ARMY. This, according to Lee, is where the network-image as not only a concept, but an art form is born. BTS videos become networked and "dismantle boundaries of media and the boundary between artist and receiver, and ultimately form a new territory of video art." Through this, the industry begins to shift and change beneath our feet to adapt to the little acknowledged network-image which BTS, and their company Big Hit, have been working towards since their inception. The community, ARMY, are an integral part of the creative process, as they are the ones who give the meaning to the content. This is a rapid decentralisation of power from the creator, as now both BTS and ARMY stand on the same plane as part of the rhizome.

From examples such as network-image we can begin to see a revolution of the status quo; BTS changing what it means to be an idol. But moreso, changing what it means to be a musician and a multi-form artist in the 21st century.

Though it has been said many times in this chapter, it will be said a few more; it takes a man to dismantle patriarchy. Or rather, a group of men. But not just any men, as has already been established. However, what is yet to be highlighted, is that these are non-dominant men. Which is to say, BTS, though men, are not Western men. They are in a unique position as Koreans to disrupt the system that seeks to uphold toxic masculine norms; they are outsiders, they are the underdogs. This is most evident when one examines their attempt to break into the Western music market; notoriously xenophobic for all the reasons we know, and more. Though it arguably needs to be men loving other men to create a revolution, it is important to note that these men need to be of difference to rattle the West to its core; only then might we change.

You see, in order for change to occur there needs to be tension, there needs to be resistance. In the case of BTS as revolutionary the root of their power lies within their nationality, and as such, their language. Though it can be argued that their music transcends language and cultural barriers as it speaks a universal love, that is simply not a belief held by all of the global West. Irrespective of how good their music might sound, or its broader commercial viability, in the U.S. in particular, BTS do not receive radio play as most of their lyrics are not in English. They are regularly asked if and when they would record an album entirely in English during interviews, the answer, unsurprisingly, is that they won't. This can be seen as their act of resistance; standing strong in their culture, in their language, and refusing to bend to the ignorant West. Instead, what they ask with this act of defiance, is for the West to rise to their level. An invitation to grow to appreciate and consume Korean language content as they have done with English and the broad reaching colonialist arm of the United States. BTS continuing to release music in their mother tongue opens many more doors; doors for other Korean cultural exports; doors for other Korean groups, and, most importantly; doors for greater love and acceptance towards the millions of American's who speak English as a second language.

It is important to note here that one cannot talk about BTS as revolutionaries without acknowledging that they are part of a much larger organisational picture. This book takes a micro look at idol limerence, with BTS as exemplars, and links the concept to a macro level, which is placing this analysis within the realms of sociology as opposed to, say, musicology. This body of work, as C. Wright Mills writes, uses a sociological imagination to understand the personal, limerence, as the political, idol. However, we must next bring into the dialogue the company who created BTS and continues to shape them to this day, Big Hit Entertainment.

On February 4, 2020, Big Hit hosted a corporate briefing with the community where they reported on 2019 achievements and their vision for the year to come. CEO Bang, introduced earlier in the book, notes that the last time they met, August 2019, they had presented Big Hit's vision of "innovating the music industry". He goes on to say that they wished to overcome the limitations of the industry and expand the entire market. Most of all, they set out to find the *Big Hit winning formula*, in the hopes that they could continue to recreate success stories like BTS' across K-pop and, as they later reported, the music industry internationally. Bang, and the rest of the company, remained adamant throughout the entire presentation, for Big Hit the fundamentals are content and fan. Further, in his closing remarks, Bang makes it clear that the three axes of Big Hit are fan, artist and company; all are regarded as equal and are valued as such.

Big Hit will innovate tours, by turning cities into BTS *tour villages* with themed hotels, sponsored drinks and meals, curated fan experiences for those who come to their shows, as well as those who do not; capturing more people than a performance alone. Through this they hope to bring the economic effect of the Seoul performances, one trillion won, to participating cities throughout the world. Through their business, beNX, two apps were developed, *Weply*, an ecommerce platform, and *Weverse*, which further centralised the power of the fan experience firmly within Big Hit. Weverse, as previously mentioned, is an app that has innovated the way fans and artists interact. Not only is it easy for the fan to connect with other fans, and the artists themselves, but the artist is afforded a streamlined experience that enables them to communicate intimately, en masse, with their fans from all around the world. President of beNX, 서우석 Seo Wooseok, reported that 1.4 million people from 205 countries access Weverse every day. He goes on to say that the secret in the success of Weverse is in "intimacy in communication between artists and fans that you could not experience anywhere else". In that sense, Big Hit are innovating ways in which parasocial interaction can be intensified, and through that, idol limerence.

There are many ways in which Big Hit are innovating, or rather, revolutionising the industry, which extend further afield than BTS alone. They are using music as a common theme to connect industries like intellectual property, literature, language education, gaming, animation, film and reality television. Through this the fan is at their core, not only as a goal but as a valued member of the process; they are revolutionising the way in which the fan is treated. Through inclusivity, Big Hit are making it easier for fans to interact with their content, and in many ways to shape it, too. No wonder, then, that Big Hit reported they nearly doubled their revenue from 2018 in 2019. With the valuing of fans comes a greater fan experience, which they will gladly pay for; they are purchasing the equivalent to emotional reciprocation, after all. Which brings back into question whether or not the fan is exploited in this binary, when they derive so much pleasure, happiness and knowledge from the experience. A company that sees the often deemed *hysterical* fans as equals is revolutionary in itself, but at the end of the day all these steps are made so that they can continue to make a profit. A complex relationship, with no right or wrong answer; the fans demand it and so they get it, Big Hit willingly obliging. Though it's not perfect, it's as close to perfect as one company can get under capitalism. After all, Big Hit, like BTS, are just a reflection of the fans; this is all of our own making and we take much delight in it.

One man, Kim Namjoon, went on a journey towards self-love; a revolution of the self. This journey filtered outwards, and influenced those closest to him, BTS. Each member continuing to define what self-love means to them. This revolution of the self turned to a revolution shared between friends, in many ways it became a revolution of loving male relationships. From there, this love was observed and experienced by their fans, ARMY, around the world; this revolution became bigger than just the group. Suddenly, it became a movement of love shared between an international community. This love was an equal exchange, of sorts, from the deeply personal level to the interpersonal to the communal, between each member of BTS and ARMY. From there it grew further outwards, to become a revolution of an industry; one which could not be achieved without the sheer mass of an all-loving ARMY, nor without the vision of the revolutionaries themselves, who represent the larger vision of Big Hit. BTS have established themselves as revolutionaries, but this is not the end of their trajectory, their story; in fact, this is just the beginning. The next step: the world, and in many ways it has already begun.

In the context of the book, a dialogue about love is not complete without limerence. You see, revolutionaries with love need those with limerence, both are necessary in the revolution; it is what truly makes this an unstoppable social movement. It is limerence, idol limerence, which is growing in number each day as more people feel the archaic call from the collective unconscious riding across the currents on the back of a *Black Swan*. It is a limerence felt towards BTS that converts a part-time listener to a full blown ARMY, ready to lead the charge in a revolution. Limerence is a love felt so potently it makes one feel as if they could change the world, as if they could save the world from itself. That is the beauty, and the sadness, of this revolution; limerence is a builder of worlds, but also a destroyer. A delicate balance between sanity and something else, we do not have all the answers yet, no one does this early on in a phenomenon. We are simply making it up as we go along, remembering to love BTS each step of the way, remembering to love ourselves through the turbulence of a one-sided love affair with an idol who doesn't know our name outside of the collective acronym.

This is a co-created revolution, made with love, made by love, made for loving. In many ways, it's a return to love as we all stand in our secret mind gardens, growing upwards amongst the flowers, towards the great expanse of the universe together. It is only between us that the universe exists, this is a revolution between BTS and ARMY; between them is all of life as we know it.

But, if a look into the life of an idol has taught us anything, it's

Revolutionary

that binaries are dangerous as the power tends to lay on one side. It's as if the binary makes the viewer need to choose between one or the other. One becomes more valued than the other, deemed lesser, which will always come second in a sentence. Or, often, the first spoken is good and the second is bad, a binary which can be neutralised with the word neutral in itself. If it's not these, it is simply something deemed as other, which still at some point is reduced to being negative, like West and East.

Wherever possible a third element must be brought in to neutralise or synthesise the power imbalance. We need to unsettle the choice so that we are able to view the two parts as intersecting, interrelated, instead of opposing parts. So what is the third aspect to BTS and ARMY, to limerence and idol limerence, to shadow and persona? The last is easy as it has already been written by Jung; shadow, and persona are neutralised by ego. More importantly, they are held in creative tension and synthesised by the collective unconscious. What neutralises the BTS and ARMY binary lacks capitalisation, but does come next on the revolutionary trajectory; it's world. It's the world that exists between BTS and ARMY which also seeks to neutralise the power imbalance, while also seeking to keep them apart; it's inherently complex. An example of what synthesises BTS and ARMY is an app such as Weverse which places, to some extent, the artist and fan on equal ground.

Lastly, to neutralise the binary of this book's own creation another trajectory must be taken into consideration: if it goes limerence to idol limerence then surely it must go from idol limerence to something post-idol limerence. It is important to note here that we are currently moving into a stage of peak idol limerence as BTS continues to grow and dominate globally, with love. What that means is that idol limerence will always exist, but exists at the expense of the fan. And, similarly, will always come at the cost of the idol's personal life. There is potential for huge growth and change under idol limerence, as we will surely see this year. However, there will come a time where greater social change simply cannot be achieved. This is when we must seek out the next stage or be doomed to repeat the cycle once more, netting more fame and fortune for the idol while more individuals fall by the wayside, unable to continue on giving all their love and energy to one group alone. That is to say, idol limerence will always exist, at the expense of others, but if a revolution is the aim, we need to move to a new way of being all together.

This post-idol limerence stage must be all powerful, in many ways it can be seen as the final piece to assemble a social movement; it is *insperence*. Within this idea is contained all the complexities of limerence and idol limerence, but also, the transformational properties needed for the revolution of our lifetime. A synthesis of this binary, of the experience of limerence, is found in this heuristic book itself. Which means that it is surely time to look towards the unknown future and dream of what happens if idol and fan meet world and transcend to a post-humanist mode of living, loving and artistic expression.

Insperence

Forever we are young, under the flower petals raining down
—Epilogue: Young Forever, BTS

When seeking to destroy Voldemort, young Harry Potter came to the bitter realisation that he had to die first before Voldemort could be vanquished. You see, Voldemort had seven Horcruxes, dark objects in which he placed a part of his soul in order to achieve immortality. Only once all seven have been destroyed does he become mortal, only then may he be killed. What Harry had only just realised was that in the act of killing his parents, Voldemort had placed a part of his soul into Harry. So, he did what any teenager would, and faced up to the most powerful dark wizard of all time; he allowed Voldemort to kill him. It is here that we find Harry in a blindingly white Kings Cross station where he is joined by the late Dumbledore.

'This is, as they say, your party,' says Dumbledore as they walk side by side.

'I expect you now realise that you and Voldemort have been connected by something other than fate.'

Harry asks if it's true, that a part of Voldemort lives within him.

Dumbledore explains that it used to, but was just destroyed

in the moments before Harry arrived at Kings Cross station; destroyed by Harry's death.

The train station is a state of limbo for Harry who now has to choose between going back, and living, or moving forward, and dying. If Harry is to live, he still must kill the final Horcrux, Voldemort's beloved snake, Nagini, before killing Voldemort himself; a seemingly impossible task. In many ways, it would be easier to die.

Dumbledore turns to leave.

Harry calls after him.

'Is this all real,' Harry pauses, 'or is it just happening inside my head?'

'Of course it's happening inside your head Harry. Why should that mean that it's not real?'

Echo watched as the city grew smaller out the plane window, smaller and smaller until the clouds swallowed the craft. She thought about how strange the sunlight was in the centre of the country, how the light made everything feel slightly wrong; like waking up and not being sure if it's early morning or late afternoon. Like the world moved without her, like she was late to a party that no one told her about and the time she had to prepare was running out. It was disorientating, Echo felt like she couldn't find her balance as the plane rocked back and forth as they turned towards the darkness; speeding towards the east coast.

At last, she was headed home.

Her face stung from where she lay her cheek on the cold train track the night before, stinging with a shame. A shame that she got to that point, and that he was there to watch it all.

She tried not to think about it, but would he have watched her die?

She shook her head.

It wasn't really RM, it wasn't Namjoon; it was just her imagination.

Insperence

Echo thought about the day she saw RM looking out at her from the mirror.

How she was unsure if it were RM or herself who she saw in the reflection, she was unsure if it was he who she loved or just a mirror image of herself in a different form.

She remembered how she felt when she broke the glass and bled.

A heavy weight on her chest, burning with embarrassment, regret. She couldn't breathe. She couldn't look herself in the eye. She didn't see him for a long time after that.

Echo couldn't find him as hard as she tried. Everywhere she looked felt like perhaps he was there just a minute ago, like he had just left the building, he had just walked by. He was time that slipped through her fingers, like water or sand. There, but ever-moving, ever-changing. There, but not hers to have, not hers to touch.

Reality was glaring Echo in the face, she knew seeing RM wasn't good for her. That it was part of a larger problem; whether it was capitalistic or psychological in nature, she remained unsure. But the fact that he haunted her, tormented her, in all his beauty and charm was unhealthy. Or rather, what truly haunted her was the endless ruminations of what he would think, what Namjoon would think of her thinking of him day in and out. That's what tormented her, seeing herself through his eyes; seeing herself as a monster.

Though she tried to keep him away, he returned again and again; she made him come back. She would miss him when he was not around, he was hard to avoid; he was everywhere she looked online. Often she swore she felt a pull from her laptop, something that would wake her with a racing heart through the night each time something happened in the fandom. Often, she felt she could anticipate his every mood.

She was tired of oscillating between the highs of loving BTS and the lows of voluntarily disempowering herself; despite BTS serving to do the opposite. If she were to just sit and listen to their lyrics, to truly take them in, she would return to empowerment. Yet if she were to try and view herself through his eyes she would punish herself, self-sabotage; she wasn't allowed to appreciate him. She convinced herself he wouldn't like it, like she was crossing a boundary by loving him without his permission.

French philosopher, Michel Foucault, studied the design of Jeremy Bentham's *Panopticon*, from which he theorised the *Panopticon Effect*. Bentham, a philosopher and theorist, didn't just write about something abstract, a panopticon is an architectural feat; it is the design of a prison guard tower. A tower placed in the middle of the prison yard, raised up so high so that the guard may stand and surveil all that must be seen, but more importantly, so that the prisoners were perpetually aware of their potential surveillance. However, according to Foucault, this means that the guard up high in the tower needn't actually be on guard, in fact, no one need be there, it could merely be the shadow of a cardboard cutout; the prisoner will act the same regardless. Whether or not the prisoner is being looked at is unverifiable, which means that, at some point, each prisoner begins to self-regulate. After some time, there would no longer be a need for a cardboard cutout, no shadow was required to instil a sense of surveillance into the prisoner. Foucault writes that those who know they are being surveilled assume a "responsibility for the constraints of power", they play the role of surveyor and the person being surveilled; they become the principle of their own subjection.

There are many ways in which this panopticon effect plays out in contemporary society, it is present especially when one begins a discourse on the literal surveillance state; cameras watch us wherever we go. A police car drives past and we check our speed, make sure we're not breaking the law, irrespective of whether or not they were looking at us. In fact, the police needn't be present any longer for us to be wary of accidentally breaking the law; many of us are so petrified of being shot we simply self-regulate to the point of staying indoors instead of taking up our human right to protest. Or, if we aren't white, and especially if we are male, we stop participating in society for fear of being shot on our way to work; the misery is that we aren't safe, even as we sit in our homes. Any time, anywhere, we may meet our death at the hands of another. As such we are on a constant edge, this is experienced on a scale unlike any other if we are in a minority group; nowhere is safe. Not even in our own minds as others' words and actions penetrate to our psyche. This is how power is asserted, this is how we, in many ways, are dominated and controlled by the state; we do it to ourselves.

This is what Echo had been doing since the first day she saw BTS, placing herself under constant surveillance; no thought went unanalysed. See, it's not just fear of violence or punishment that causes us to self-regulate. We internalise dominant discourses and use them as a social checklist, of sorts, to gauge our relevancy, our morality and our ability to be accepted by society on any given day.

What makes BTS so popular lies within their talent, their musicality, their dance, their stages, their production, their aesthetics, their lyrics, their artistry, their character, their message, their culture; the list goes on. This is a list of what draws ARMY, and the rest of the world near. But BTS are not without criticism, for every ARMY there are five more people being homophobic, xenophobic and increasingly judgemental. This, in part, is due to the dominant discourse that BTS are serving to disrupt. A discourse that says men have to look and act a certain way, a discourse that says what pop music must look and sound like, a discourse that reduces the emotions of fans to an unacceptable female hysteria; for every reason ARMY has for loving BTS, there is a discourse that stands in opposition to it. Loving BTS is a radical act of defiance, but the act in itself does not cancel out the discourse in the minds of the fans and onlookers. hooks writes that love is more than an emotion, it's an action. It is here that we can see love as an action, as a perpetual act of resistance. An act which tempers the negativity through a daily recommitment to the movement, to the revolution which starts, and ends, with an outpouring of love between BTS and ARMY.

On top of these discourses, or rather, sitting alongside them, are the other discourses that serve to dominate and control the minds of people, in particular, minorities, around the world. This is where we can begin to see the intersection of BTS, ARMY and world; this is where the complexities multiply. So, if we are to take one common discourse used in dialogue about BTS, that of a hysterical female fan, and add it to a discourse prevalent in the world more broadly, obsession, madness: what loving BTS suddenly becomes is a question of sanity. To add to the complexity is the existence of a kind of love that is not commonly discussed, nor acknowledged, limerence, which the literature often still refers to as a mental illness. Mental illness which we are told, as evident by the name, is an ailment. It's something wrong that must be fixed so that we can better work, so that we can go back to cranking the capitalist machine more efficiently.

This is the discourse that Echo internalised, the one of madness, that loving someone from afar without their permission is immoral. So she began to police herself, punish herself for the thoughts that she could not entirely control, as they came from deep within the collective unconscious. She punished herself the only way she knew how; to deny herself of the things that made her happy. These same things were what drove the limerence to new heights, the limerence in itself made it impossible to truly rid herself of the very subject matter that triggered the need for surveillance. She was so concerned with becoming truly mad that, through her own efforts to stop, she brought it on and drove herself to the brink of despair, and beyond. The panopticon effect resulted in Echo's perpetual disempowerment; she was regulating thoughts no one else could see or hear and believed herself to be something other than sane. This is how power is exerted in contemporary times, how the masses are controlled. They are told they are mad, that madness is inherently wrong, and through this, they become disempowered. The last thing capitalism needs is those experiencing a different reality feeling empowered; you cannot control someone who is equal parts mad and able to step into their power, whatever that may be.

"I would like to begin by talking about myself."

Namjoon stands in front of the United Nations General Assembly in New York, it's September 24 2018. Just 12 days earlier he had celebrated his 24th birthday, now he was delivering a career-defining speech with BTS by his side.

"In an intro to one of our early albums, there is a line that says, *my heart stopped... I was maybe nine or ten.*"

Echo sat in the window seat as the plane began to descend into her city. Her hand clamped over her mouth as she watched Namjoon on the screen before her talking about the time his heart stopped beating. This wasn't the first time she had seen the video, but it hit differently this time. He, too, had internalised many ideas about who or what he should be. He, too, had spent a long time viewing himself through the eyes of others.

"No one called out my name, and neither did I. My heart stopped and my eyes closed shut. So, like this, I, we, all lost our names. We became like ghosts."

Cut.

Echo was back in South Australia, in the bitter cold. The train sped past her face once again, with each gush of air between carriages she was cast further back in time. RM still standing on the other side, watching, waiting; he knew she'd be back.

Cut.

She walked side by side with Narcissus as they painted their future together, the sun dipping lower in the sky. Echo knew she wouldn't have much time left with him, that this was the moment where she professed her eternal love. This was the moment he said nothing, looking away instead of saying "I love you, too". He never said he'd tell her he loved her when he reached the East coast, that's just what Echo told herself to make it feel better; she told herself he was coming for her, when he wasn't. He never planned to be with her forever.

Echo's heart contorted, knowing this was their last moment together.

Out of the corner of her eye she could see RM nearby, reading a book on a bench.

Cut.

Echo stood out in front of a floor length mirror in her bedroom, picking out which dress she would greet Narcissus in at the airport. Singing, swaying from side to side as she daydreamed about what they'd do, all the places they would go.

She held her phone up to her ear, a call from the West coast.

He was gone, said the voice.

He didn't want this world anymore; he died three times on the operating table.

Echo sunk down, she hadn't thought of this day in a long time.

Namjoon said his heart stopped when he was maybe nine or ten, Echo's stopped right then and there as she screamed until she couldn't any longer.

She looked up, RM in the mirror, staring back at her.

Cut.

A blur of memories sped past her eyes as the train carriage snaked past; her life as a ghost started the day Narcissus died.

Cut.

Echo sat on her bed as *Idol* played before her eyes, larger than life. She became human the day she answered the call of the collective unconscious and returned to a place of love, the day she first saw, and returned to, Bangtan.

For the first time in a long time, as the colours of the music video exploded and her pupils expanded in delight, she was safe. It was euphoric, transcendent; she hadn't felt a love like this before. Her spirit rushed back to her body and she was born anew, a clean slate on which to build a persona that could take her where she wanted to go; a one way ticket to BTS.

Insperence

You know, Echo thought to herself, *if this is who I am I think I'm ok with it.*

She thought back to how having her heart broken by Felix led her to a new love; sociology. How she felt when she first read excerpts from *Das Kapital* and felt her understanding of the world expand. How she felt when Durkheim's theory of religion made her think of how she idolised musicians; how music is the religion of the 21st century. In those moments she was truly happy.

In her mind she saw her younger self, embarrassed to be in a pretty dress in Hattie's garden. She remembered how she felt she didn't measure up. How she was so mortified by her own body that she rejected it until it no longer existed.

She placed that younger self next to the Echo who stood triumphant on the podium after her first powerlifting competition, a medal around her neck.

"Your body," younger Echo exclaimed, looking up from second place to older Echo who stood on first, "it's so... different."

Older Echo looked down at her legs, thinking.

"I still have a long way to go," she wrapped her arm around younger Echo and smiled.

"I want to be strong like you."

Older Echo laughed, loud.

"Oh, you will be. In many ways you already are."

There, on third place, a teenage Echo stood in all her angst-ridden glory, mouth agape at the room before her.

"Where am I?" she whispered.

"You're thirteen years in the future," university Echo leaned over to whisper, "future Echo just won a powerlifting competition."

"Sport?" teenage Echo mused, "you've changed."

Echo sighed.

"It's hardly a sport, I just stand in one place and flex."

"Ah," teenage Echo giggled, "that makes more sense."

She looked at Echo's legs, raising an eyebrow.

"Echo... did you not become a writer?"

"Oh, but she is!" exclaimed university Echo, "after this competition she is flying to a national writers' residency."

Teenage Echo smiled big.

"Shit yeah."

"Language," Echo warned.

Teenage Echo rolled her eyes.

"Just don't write something soppy about Narcissus, okay? Write something weird and gross so the other writers are intimidated by you. That's what I'd do."

Echo paused, smiling.

"Consider it done."

University Echo looked around at the room, taking in the colourful plates and barbells that glinted in the light of cameras flashing.

"You really did it, you know?" she said.

"What do you mean?"

"You became who we dreamed of being."

The room swirled about Echo, her other selves disappearing before her eyes. *Idol* still playing in the background. She paused to think, soaking up the warmth from her memory of BTS.

I've come a long way, I trust myself.

She closed her eyes.

I know what to do now, she smiled, her heart twisting in her chest.

Cut.

Echo looked around, she was back on the plane. It was rapidly descending as alarm bells sounded throughout the cabin.

She stood in the aisle between seats, unsure how she got there.

Right there, before her very eyes...

Namjoon.

"Are you on board?"

He winked.

Echo frowned.

Her heart was racing but she remained confused.

It was Namjoon, with light brown hair that fell over his forehead. In street clothes, a jacket and a beanie.

It was him.

It worked.

But did it?

"What?" she said, shrill, in shock.

"For the revolution."

He winked again.

"This must be some kind of sick joke."

"Get it?" he points to the cabin.

"On board... we're on board a plane..."

Echo's eyes rolled around in her head from the hilarity.

"Ha, I get it," she said dryly.

"What's wrong?"

"You're Namjoon."

Namjoon looked down at himself.

"That's right."

"You're usually RM."

He mashed his lips together, thinking.

"You're right."

"Say something in Korean. If it's really you, say something in Korean that I don't know. Anything. Say it."

Namjoon paused, eyes moving from side to side.

"You won't, will you? I have no concept of your language, so I'm making you speak English. You're still just a figure of my imagination."

Namjoon fell silent, looking down at the ground.

"Namjoon," Echo called out, the distance between them grew as the plane became twice as long.

Why is it Namjoon for the first time?

Echo paused to think. There had to be a way to see if her theory was correct, if it was working.

A beat.

A beat.

Idol Limerence

A beat.

Echo wouldn't be surprised if RM materialised to watch the astral leaps she was making as she shuffled through all her knowledge on limerence and persona to be twice as sure. But RM wasn't there, that was the point; it was a breakthrough she was having after all, not a breakdown.

Echo lifted her foot and took a long step forward.

Namjoon blinked.

She took another.

Echo looked at the empty blue chairs that surrounded them.

Pink, she nodded.

They turned pink.

Namjoon's eyebrows rose, impressed.

"Theory, confirmed," Echo whispered to herself.

"Pardon?"

Namjoon now stood right before her, this was the closest they had ever been.

Echo took a deep breath, trying not to squeal with excitement; she couldn't believe he was finally there.

Now wasn't the time for gushing.

"We have to talk," Echo said, pursed lips.

"Are we not talking right now?"

Echo rolled her eyes.

"I know how to make it stop, the limerence. I know how to make you go away."

Namjoon nodded, in thought.

"The answer was here all along," he smiled, "wasn't it?"

Echo sighed.

"Yeah."

"Per-so-na," he said, the same way he did in the song.

"Who the hell am I?" Echo replied.

Jung describes the process of divesting oneself from the wrappings of a persona as *individuation*. He writes that through this process one is also divested of "primordial images" which hold

Insperence

suggestive power over the consciousness. Further, the unconscious acts automatically and extends the range of consciousness. It is suggested that the process of individuation brings about greater self-awareness, which in turn begins to remove the layer of one's consciousness which has been "superimposed over the collective unconscious". It is theorised in this book that the unconscious is also where limerence comes from, especially idol limerence which calls one back to the collective unconscious. Not only does this further demonstrate the link between persona and limerence, but it shows how one can disintegrate a persona, remove it, take it away. As such, theoretically, we could take away the limerence, too.

The process in which individuation can occur involves stepping into our own fantasies and acting them out as if they are completely real. This is what Echo attempted by turning the chairs pink, proving to herself that Namjoon was indeed appearing before her because she had consciously delved deep enough into her unconscious that she was able to summon him instead of RM. RM, as a persona, was appearing to her as a part of an uncontrollable limerence, she couldn't find Namjoon as she wasn't properly acting in her own fantasy state; she didn't believe it was real and became passive, disempowered, despite often acting with a degree of autonomy. In this case, RM was operating, as idol limerence theory suggests, as a persona which is a proxy for Namjoon which allows him to love millions without destroying himself in the process. Further, RM acted as a portal between limerence and idol limerence, between Echo and Namjoon so that, if they were both willing, they might go on towards insperence together.

Jung explains that if one's unconscious mind has power over the conscious — in this case, when the limerence has power over the conscious — the strength of the limerence here can be diminished through funneling conscious energy into the production of fantasies. Which is to mean, one must happen *to* their fantasies, instead of letting the fantasies happening to them in a passive state. Through this one's conscious horizons are expanded by growing an awareness of other unconscious thoughts, feelings and memories. Over time this begins to shift the dominance of the unconscious; and as such, limerence.

Lastly, idol limerence can be seen as a call to one's own destiny, a returning to love. Aided by the collective unconscious, groups like BTS trigger certain predetermined blueprints in their fans through the use of archetypes and symbols. The quest of idol limerence can also be seen, according to Willmott and Bentley, as a journey "towards authenticity". So not only can one divest themselves of their persona to remove the limerence, but the limerence, in theory, can also fade as one fully accepts themselves and aligns with their destiny; whatever that may be.

"So what do I do?" Echo looked down at her feet, "Do I end the limerence, or do I become a revolutionary?"

Namjoon tapped her foot with his, they were both wearing converse.

"Isn't that for you to decide?"

Echo paused.

"I'm scared it's already too late."

"What do you mean?"

"I had to enter the process of losing you just to have this conversation," Echo looked around, "if I stay much longer I fear when I wake you will be gone forever and I will be someone else entirely."

Namjoon looked down at her, blinking slowly, thinking.

"You didn't need to come in here to find me."

"But I did," Echo's throat clenched as she held back tears, "this isn't sustainable, this limerence. If it's not sustainable for me, then imagine how many others are suffering? There has to be another answer, but we have to find it together."

He waited for her to regain her composure.

"That kind of makes you the superhero of this story," he laughed, "I've been waiting for you, Anpanman!"

Echo smiled, he was funny.

They fell silent again, unsure what to do or say next.

"Can you see me?" Echo whispered, "am I in your head just like you're in mine?"

"I can see you," he rubbed his face with his hand, "but I don't think we're in our heads."

"Where are we then?" Echo looked up, eyes meeting his, "are we on the spiritual plane, in the other world?"

Namjoon laughed.

"If we were in your theorised *other world* we wouldn't be doing this right now," he grinned.

"What would we be doing then?" Echo asked, wide eyed.

A smile slowly started to creep across Namjoon's face, his eyes didn't leave hers.

Echo's heart fluttered.

"Oh," her cheeks flushed red, "well then. I mean, it's just a theory," she laughed.

They looked down at their shoes again.

"So where are we?"

"I don't know, but it feels like we're headed for something big."

"Do you know how long I've been trying to see you?" Echo asked as she looked up at him.

"What do you mean?"

"I've been talking to RM this whole time, and I've got to be honest, he does more staring than talking."

"Ah," Namjoon laughed, his smile occupying more than half his face, "I've been busy, sorry."

"So what do you think? Am I out of my mind?"

Namjoon looked around again as sunlight began to filter through the empty cabin, still hurtling towards the ground.

"I think we're far beyond your mind now."

"How much do you know?"

Namjoon blinked.

"I want to know how much you know. In real life. Not wherever we are now. Have you reached the same conclusions that I have?"

The distance between them started to grow.

Echo's heart sunk.

She wasn't going to get her answer, not like this.

"Hey," Namjoon laughed, "hey Echo... I know how you can decide."

"How?"

He pointed to the sun rising on the horizon.

"What lights you up?"

Echo blinked and they were standing on the edge of the wing, time standing still as the sun rose over the ocean stretched out all around them.

Echo turned away from the blinding sun to look at Namjoon again, the light casting long golden beams over his face.

He smiled again.

"What lights you up, Echo?"

His smile began to fade, his eyes grew larger in anticipation.

Echo paused in thought.

"It's y-"

She stopped.

RM stood before her in the place Namjoon once was.

Well? He pressed, *are you going to answer him?*

The turbulence rattled Echo from side to side.

She was back in her seat, Namjoon still on the screen before her delivering his speech.

"Tell me your story. I want to hear your voice, and I want to hear your conviction."

Her eyes fluttered while she intently watched the screen, it jostled as the wheels hit the tarmac.

"Speak Yourself."

Okay, Echo thought as the cabin filled with life and movement, *I think I will.*

The final stage of idol limerence, the stage that comes before

Insperence

insperence, is idol limerence as a choice. A conscious choice made by the person experiencing limerence can be made at any stage in the process, as, once again, it is not experienced linearly. However, for insperence to be reached, a choice *for* idol limerence must be made. Which is to say, limerence is out of the control of the experiencer, something that happens *to* them. Idol limerence in its full and final form is, to a degree, an equal give and take between *to* and *from*; the limerent is able to shape their experience in one way or another. Insperence, however, is an experience that exists *with*, *between*, *from*, *to* and *for* all parties involved. Insperence fully aligns with the cosmic love that Buber talks about as it exists in between many, instead of to and from a binary of idol and fan. In another sense, insperence is the merging of a binary into a spiritual, transcendent *one*; a return to love in its pure form, the radiant light of the sun or its reflection on the moon. Love, in its purest form, is light.

It must also be noted here that the idea of limerence is a past understanding still relevant today, idol limerence is a contemporary reimagining and insperence is future; it is largely unknown and yet to be experienced. Therefore it is hard to define, as we cannot fully define the future; we cannot hold the future, nor will we ever. Perhaps that is the beauty of the future, and insperence, it's ever-changing and holds all the answers; something we can strive towards for the rest of our days. If anything, insperence is transformational and transcendent; how this may look is up to interpretation. We will only truly know when we look back in the years to come what shape it takes.

There are many reasons why one might make a choice for idol limerence, and it is argued that fans around the world make this choice day in and out without any knowledge on the subject. You see, idol limerence, for many, is the safe-love alternative for a generation burdened with saving the world. A generation having to come to terms with the fact that they may already be too late, a generation that feels largely powerless but wholly responsible for our collective future. Though the vast majority of the generation in question may be millennials, this particular generation is more a generation of thought as opposed to age.

What idol limerence offers people is the ability to experience, give and receive love in a controlled environment. No rejection, no heartbreak; it's just love, safe, euphoric love. A dynamic love that grows and changes over time. A love that fulfills, to some degree, one's yearning for another, and allows them to focus more fully on the task at hand, whatever that may be. It provides comfort, transient relief, and with it comes a community of people feeling the same way, people who could perhaps become friends or family over time.

The existence of idol limerence as a safe-love alternative is not to say that individuals are without love, or cannot enter into or maintain loving intimate relationships. Rather, that the heart has a huge capacity for love, and that idol limerence is a way for many to give and receive love without, or outside of, the turbulence of interpersonal relationships. Further, it is not to say that a choice for idol limerence, and through that, the experience of insperence is an action against love with others. Rather, it sits alongside each person's narrative, it's a highly subjective experience and will look different on an individual basis. In some cases, idol limerence can be a highly inspirational force which many turn to in order to drive their creative process, such as writing a book. The most common example of this is using an idol as muse, capitalising on the outpouring of love and romantic inclinations we make in our idol's direction to channel into creating art in whatever form it may take. Artists with muses are not without other romantic relationships, rather this particular relationship is entered into equal parts willingly and often, to a degree, out of our control as we surrender to desire in its many forms.

Zygmunt Bauman, a Polish-British sociologist and philosopher, writes that we are now living in late modernity, as opposed to having moved through modernity to postmodernity. Modernity refers to a period of time where society shifted towards a different way of thinking, and as such, a different mode of operation deemed to be *modern*. Modernity, in many ways, encapsulates a shift in ethos, philosophy and the formation of social science as a school of thought and study. Further, modernity is linked to the rise of capitalism and decline of secularisation. Late modernity is a continuation of modernity, ever-changing social and political landscapes as we hurtle into the future. Bauman refers to late modernity as *liquid modernity*, which is to say, that modernity in the here and now is about the individual. Who or what the individual may be is in a constant state of flux, perpetually changing as traditional social patterns are replaced by self-chosen ones; all that was once solid now turns to liquid. The pressure which liquid modernity places on the individual is huge, they must somehow intuit their future and make adjustments every single day to ensure the viability of their chosen path. Historically, the social focus has been on staying: one job, one car, one house, one family, one dream. Now, the onus is on the individual to shift rather than stay, which can result in a variety of existential tortures; much like the torture of Echo's own making as she shifts her liquid persona to align with her hopes and dreams.

Simone de Beauvoir, a French writer, feminist, social theorist and existential philosopher, explores similar themes in her book *The Ethics of Ambiguity*. de Beauvoir writes that we, humans, are fundamentally free and that this freedom comes from our nothingness. This nothingness is an important element to being self-aware and is at the heart of humankind, the heart which consists of consciousness we have of ourselves. Further, to add complexity, we are both subject and object, just like the idol; we are free and tactic at the same time. In our freedom we are able to observe ourselves, choose what to do. In our tactility we are immobilised by our physical selves, social constraints and political powers.

Idol Limerence

Both the work of de Beauvoir, from 1947, and Bauman, from 2000, serves to illustrate the pain and beauty of human existence; painfully self-aware while the future remains beautifully unknown. It is only through this pain can we truly be free, through the tension created under negotiating the ambivalence we feel towards an ambiguous future. For many, the pain is too much, which we see as a broader societal malaise. Action towards an unknown future without leadership or guidance is no easy task, yet it is a path many of us must perpetually walk under liquid modernity. Perhaps it is this liquid modernity which is the ocean in which an idol drowns as they show us the way forward.

Idol limerence exists as a result of liquid modernity, created as a way to negotiate the ambivalence we individually and collectively feel towards an ambiguous future; liquid limerence, if you like. Idol groups such as BTS provide entertainment, transient relief, a portal to a new world. They give us an avenue to experience a kind of safe-love, even if it is primarily inside our own minds, through which we can imagine and recreate ourselves. But it is also BTS who are moving beyond idol limerence, as they transcend their own societal and cultural constraints. This asks of ARMY the huge task of holding tensions in their own lives as they negotiate the dangerous discourses that exist to exert dominance and control over all, especially women and minorities. For some, this is too much, which we see manifested as outrage towards BTS for not being what idols should be, or historically have been. For BTS breaking the mould is asking the audience to do the same, and some simply cannot keep up, nor do they have to.

Both the experience of idol limerence and the ambivalence brought about by liquid modernity can be summarised in the following passage by de Beauvoir:

> I should like to be the landscape which I am contemplating, I should like this sky, this quiet water to think themselves within me, that it

Insperence

might be I whom they express in flesh and bone, and I remain at a distance. But it is also by this distance that the sky and the water exist before me. My contemplation is an excruciation only because it is also a joy. I can not appropriate the snow field where I slide. It remains foreign, forbidden, but I take delight in this very effort toward an impossible possession.

The idol, like the future, can only be experienced at a distance. For when we are face to face with an idol, we are merely two humans. When we are face to face with the future it is merely just the present; tomorrow never truly comes. We cannot appropriate the idol, nor the future, we can never hold them in our hands. Yet idol limerence seeks out this possession, knowing that it can never be so; that is the pain and beauty of this relationship. Though it is safe, it is not without torment or suffering, and yet it is welcomed; this is how we balance the ambivalence we feel towards the future. All our hope lies with someone who will live forever in their words, in their music, the same words and music that heals us, makes us and transforms us. We want it, but we cannot have it; an exquisite pain. The burden of a revolutionary. Under this tension we bloom until we ache.

Insperence is a state of perpetual inspiration which is experienced alongside feelings of limerence. Where the feelings of anxiety due to unequal communications lessen, and love in its purest state is able to freely flow amongst all experiencing limerence, not just between two parties. It is here where BTS and ARMY are deconstructed and reconstructed as true equals that radical social change is possible. For the very act of stepping towards recreating an idol group and their fan group as absolute equals, irrespective of how that may look, is radical social change in itself.

This is not to say that insperence cancels out the complexities of male/female, master/slave, powerful/powerless relationships which the current idol/fan binary can be seen as, rather, insperence provides space to heal these binaries. Insperence does not hold the answers, rather it holds the space in which answers can arise from a dialogue between equals. Only through active, equal participation between BTS and ARMY can the power dynamics shift, but both parties can never truly exist outside of their global context. Yet right there is one of the societal barriers that will slowly be chipped away at if BTS and ARMY meet as equals; that will be social change in and of itself. From there, systems can be changed, societal norms reimagined, anything is possible. This can only begin to be dreamed of, talked of, worked towards, if they are true equals, not idol and fan but something else entirely.

It is also important to add here that insperence is characterised by a move further into the realms of post-humanism. Buber was originally used to show a spiritual understanding of being, that being exists relationally; which is echoed in the work of Heidegger. However, many do not see this as post-human, though it is argued that seeing love as a universal, comic force is quite outside the realms of humanity. As such, a move towards post-humanism will involve a move to the *Chthulucene* which post-human ecofeminist Donna Haraway originated to encapsulate "past, present, and to come". Chthulucene, according to Haraway, is to capture the "dynamic ongoing sym-chthonic forces and powers of which people are a part, within which ongoingness is at stake." Haraway writes that perhaps "with intense commitment and collaborative work and play with other terrans, flourishing for rich multispecies assemblages that include people will be possible." That is to say, insperence is a refocusing of the revolutionary journey to include more than the anthropocene, it needs to include *all* of existence in order for true change to occur. BTS may already be revolutionising the human world, but it is far more than just humans and the built environment that stands between us. We are not just reflections of our other bodies and the buildings they made; we are a reflection of mother nature and father sky. We must inevitably return to our higher purpose of loving each other, while remembering that humans are not the only 'other' in existence, far from it.

For the time being, insperence is only attributed to BTS, the revolutionaries in the idol limerence realm. Insperence requires the idols to not be passive in the limerence. Rather, they are vocal actors who drive and shape the limerent experience through the collective unconscious as co-creators with their fans. Insperence is harmony between idol and limerent, where both experience a feeling of limerence towards the other.

Idol limerence is BTS and ARMY taking a step towards one another, insperence is when they leap together. Theoretically, if idol limerence can bridge the minds of idol and limerent, allowing the limerent to travel to the new world and see their idol in visions, then the idol can do and see the same. That is to say, they both can meet one another on this fantasy bridge between worlds, outside of space and time, to relay information pertinent to their lives on the physical realm. It's not just the limerent who can see the idol, just like legilimens, the visions could very well go both ways. Instead of madness, it is something else entirely. What exactly it is can only be known once the leap occurs, and both the experience of idol and fan, or rather, the two limerents is properly examined side by side. This book has been just one side of the idol limerence picture, from the perspective of the collective fan. The answers also lie within the mind, and experience, of the idol; only then may we begin to know what insperence could look like.

The future, like insperence, is unknown. What is known, however, is that BTS and ARMY have the most capacity, ability, to take this leap together. Though they are not currently equals, they are very close. All it will take is for both parties to meet as collaborators, to remove the binary of idol and fan; to meet as true equals, embodied humans. Humans who are very much a part of their social and cultural context, but humans in limerence and love; open and willing to change the world together. It will start from a conversation, a thought, an idea. Through love as an action it will rise, and the rest will become history.

"Namjoon."

It's late afternoon in autumn, the sun filtering through the trees as it slowly sets. The air was cold, the beams of sunlight providing fleeting warmth and illumination.

No one else was in the park, the hum of the city could be heard beyond the forest.

Echo walked towards Namjoon as he stared up at an old tree, his eyes searching for answers in its branches that spread upwards towards the sky.

He turned around, surprised to see her there.

"오랜만이에요," Namjoon grinned.

Echo's eyes nearly fell out of her head as she stopped dead in her tracks.

"Did you..." she started.

His eyebrows raised.

"Did I?" she shook her head.

"You've been learning Korean," he walked towards Echo.

"Yes. But I didn't learn that," she said slowly, looking up at him, confused.

He smiled.

"Maybe I'm not a figure of your imagination, after all," he winked.

Echo tried to speak but no words came out.

"I'm sorry!" he exclaimed, "I shouldn't mess with you like that, I couldn't help myself."

He turned her around so they could walk in the same direction.

"Are you well?" he asked, hands behind his back as he walked in step with Echo.

"Mm," Echo thought, "yes, very well thank you. That's why I'm here."

"Not because you missed me?"

Insperence

Echo rolled her eyes.

"I've figured out the next step in your trajectory," she paused, "in our trajectory."

"We have a trajectory?"

"Of course," Echo laughed softly, "I had to plan it all out before I came back to tell you about it."

"Do you mean..." Namjoon dragged his words out, "you'll be a revolutionary with me?"

Echo stopped causing Namjoon to have to double back.

"Oh, yes! I will!" Echo clapped her hands together, "sorry, I forgot to tell you. I've been busy."

"We all have your BTS blog bookmarked, we know you've been busy," he sighed, "keep talking."

Echo wrinkled her nose, but complied.

"I know how to move through limerence to a new state where we, and everyone else, can be revolutionaries. I think it's the only way for BTS and ARMY to survive. I call it..." she paused.

Namjoon mimed a drumroll.

"Insperence."

"Oh, like inspiration and limerence?"

Echo frowned.

"Legilimens goes both ways, baby," he winked.

Echo sighed.

"Anyway," she started to walk again, "we have to meet. I need to know what the real you knows."

Namjoon pulled her backwards by her jacket.

"What do you mean?"

"We have to meet. As equals."

Echo stood with her back to Namjoon, his hand still on her jacket.

She could feel him thinking as the sun dipped lower, she looked to their shadow but only saw one.

"As equals," he repeated.

He knew what she had meant.

Echo faced Namjoon, sunlight shining from behind his head

like a halo.

Soft footsteps sounded from behind her.

She turned around.

"You're here," she said. Breathless. Surprised.

I wouldn't miss it, he replied.

Echo stepped back so she could see them both, now standing between RM and Namjoon.

"We meet as equals," she repeated to them both.

"And then?"

"We leap."

Epilogue: 7

Referenced Works

Words

Bauman, Z. (2000). *Liquid modernity*. Polity.

Bennett, N., Rossmeisl, A., Turner, K., Holcombe, B., Young, R., Brown, T., & Key, H. (2017). *Parasocial relationships: The nature of celebrity fascinations*. <https://www.findapsychologist.org/parasocial-relationships-the-nature-of-celebrity-fascinations/>

Bruner, R. (2019). *The mastermind behind BTS opens up about making a K-Pop juggernaut*. <https://time.com/5681494/bts-bang-si-hyuk-interview/>

BTS Dicon. (2018). *Behind the scene BTS*. Vol. 2. (Trans. doyoubangtan). <https://doyoubangtan.wordpress.com/2018/04/20/translation-of-dispatch-dicons-bts-interview-bts-the-road-to-the-sea/>

Buber, M. (1996). *I and Thou*. (Trans. W. Kaufmann). Touchstone.

Choi, M. (2018). *Economic effects of BTS: K-Pop group BTS induces production worth 4 tril. won per year*. <http://www.businesskorea.co.kr/news/articleView.html?idxno=27583>

Connect, BTS. (2020). *Connect, BTS*. <https://www.connect-bts.com/>

de Beauvoir, S. (1997). *The ethics of ambiguity*. (Trans. B. Frechtman). Citadel Press.

Eagleman, D. (2019). *The creative brain*. Netflix.

Elfving-Hwang, J. (2018). K-Pop idols, artificial beauty and affective fan relationships in South Korea. In A. Elliot, (Ed.), *Routledge handbook of celebrity studies*. Routledge.

Foucault, F. (1977). *Discipline and punish*. (Trans. A. Sheridan). Pantheon Books.

Giddens, A. (1992). *The transformation of intimacy: Sexuality, love and eroticism in modern societies*. Polity.

Giddens, A. (1991). *Modernity and self-identity: Self and society in the late modern age*. Polity.

Giggins, A., Eaglehawk, W., & Williams, K. (2020). *BTS are the world's most revolutionary artists right now: Here's why it's making people uncomfortable*. <https://www.helloasia.com.au/features/bts-are-the-worlds-most-revolutionary-artists-right-now-heres-why-its-making-people-uncomfortable/>

Goffman, E. (1959). *The presentation of self in everyday life*. Doubleday Anchor.

Haraway, D. (2015). Anthropocene, Capitalocene, Plantationocene, Chthulucene: Making kin. *Environmental Humanities*. 6, 159-165.

Heidegger, M. (2010). *Being and time*. (Trans. J. Stambaugh). State University of New York Press.

hooks, b. (2001). *All about love: New visions*. Harper Perennial.

IZE. (2019). *BTS pledges to 'tell the story of our generation with our lyrics'*. <http://www.ize.co.kr/articleView.html?no=2019040102057238751&page=7>

Jung, C. (1967). *Two essays on analytical psychology*. Princeton University Press.

Kim, Y. (2019). *BTS the review: A comprehensive look at the music of BTS*. (Trans. H.J. Chung). RH Korea.

Lee, J. (2019). *BTS and ARMY culture*. (Trans. O. Han & S. Park). Communication Books.

Lee, J. (2019). *BTS, art revolution*. (Trans. S. Kim, M. Chae, J. Won & S. Lee). Parrhesia Publishers.

Marx, K. (1977). *Capital*. (Trans. B. Fowkes). Kopf Doubleday.

Mead, G. (1934). *Mind, self and society*. University of Chicago Press.

Mills, C. W. (1959). *The sociological imagination*. Oxford University Press.

Novak, M. (2013). *The myth of romantic love and other essays*. Transaction Publishers.

Ponchowearingpinocchio. (2018). *Stolen*. <https://archiveo-

Referenced Works

fourown.org/works/17048093>

Romano, A. (2018). *How K-Pop became a global phenomenon.* <https://www.vox.com/culture/2018/2/16/16915672/what-is-kpop-history-explained>

Seabrook, J. (2012). *Factory girls: Cultural technology and the making of K-Pop.* <http://www.newyorker.com/magazine/2012/10/08/factory-girls-2>

Simonelli, D. (2012). *Working class heroes: Rock music and British society in the 1960s and 1970s.* Lexington Books.

Tennov, D. (1979). *Love and limerence: The experience of being in love.* Scarborough House.

Wakin, A., & Vo, D. (2008). *Love-variant: The Wakin-Vo I.D.R. model of limerence.* <http://citeseerx.ist.psu.edu/viewdoc/download?doi=10.1.1.729.1932&rep=rep1&type=pdf>

Willmott, L., & Bentley, E. (2015). *Exploring the lived-experience of limerence: A journey toward authenticity.* <https://nsuworks.nova.edu/tqr/vol20/iss1/2/>

Yonhap. (2019). *BTS' latest three concerts in Seoul had economic effect of W1tr: report.* <http://www.koreaherald.com/view.php?ud=20191223000424>

Music

Aoki, S., Conrad, N., RM, Torrey, J., Wells, A., Spreckley, R., & Slow Rabbit. (2018). 전하지 못한 진심 (The Truth Untold). Recorded by BTS. *Love Yourself 結 Answer.* Big Hit Entertainment.

BTS. (2013). Intro: 2 cool 4 skool ft. DJ Fritz. Recorded by BTS. *2 cool 4 skool.* Big Hit Entertainment.

DJ Swivel, Audien, Sunshine, Zelmani, E., RM, Tanner, W., Dalhqvist, G., Sosa, C., Suga, j-hope, Elohim, Armato, A., Karlsson, A., Viktorovich, A. (2020). We Are Bulletproof: The Eternal. Recorded by BTS. *Map of the soul: 7.* Big Hit Entertainment.

Girelli, C., j-hope, Hyun, L., RM, & "Hitman" Bang. (2019). Heartbeat. Recorded by BTS. *BTS world: Original soundtrack*. Big Hit Entertainment.

Hiss Noise, RM, & Pdogg. (2019). Intro: Persona. Recorded by BTS. *Map of the soul: Persona*. Big Hit Entertainment.

Hiss Noise, Supreme Boi, & j-hope. (2020). Outro: Ego. Recorded by BTS. *Map of the soul: 7*. Big Hit Entertainment.

"Hitman" Bang, Djan, R.M., Slow Rabbit, RM, & Foster, A. (2018). Serendipity. Recorded by BTS. *Love Yourself 結 Answer*. Big Hit Entertainment.

"Hitman" Bang, Pdogg, & RM. (2018). Fake love. Recorded by BTS. *Love yourself 結 Answer*. Big Hit Entertainment.

Pdogg, Brother Su, "Hitman" Bang, RM, Suga, j-hope, & Slow Rabbit. (2016). Whalien 52. Recorded by BTS. *The most beautiful moment in life: Young forever*. Big Hit Entertainment.

Pdogg, & RM. (2013). Intro: O!RUL8,2?. Recorded by BTS. *O!RUL8,2?*. Big Hit Entertainment.

Pdogg, RM, Rigo, A, Nantes, V., & Kelly, C. (2020). Black swan. Recorded by BTS. *Map of the soul: 7*. Big Hit Entertainment.

Pdogg, Slow Rabbit, RM, Suga, & j-hope. (2014). Intro: Skool luv affair. Recorded by BTS. *Skool luv affair*. Big Hit Entertainment.

RM & Perry, C. J. (2018). Singularity. Recorded by BTS. *Love yourself 結 Answer*. Big Hit Entertainment.

Slow Rabbit, RM, & Hiss Noise. (2018). Trivia 承: Love. Recorded by BTS. *Love yourself 結 Answer*. Big Hit Entertainment.

Slow Rabbit, RM, "Hitman" Bang, Suga, & j-hope. (2016). Epilogue: Young forever. Recorded by BTS. *The most beautiful moment in life: Young forever*. Big Hit Entertainment.

Suga, El Capitxn, Ghstloop, Pdogg, & RM. (2020). Interlude: Shadow. Recorded by BTS. *Map of the soul: 7*. Big Hit Entertainment.

Referenced Works

Movies

Black Swan. Dir. Darren Aronofsky, Fox Searchlight Pictures, 2010.
Donnie Darko. Dir. Richard Kelly, Pandora Cinema, 2001.
Eternal Sunshine of the Spotless Mind. Dir. Michel Gondry, Focus Features, 2004.
Harry Potter and the Deathly Hallows Part 2. Dir. David Yates, Warner Bros. Pictures, 2011.
Her. Dir. Spike Jonze, Warner Bros. Pictures, 2013.
Moulin Rouge! Dir. Baz Luhrmann, 20th Century Fox, 2001.
Romeo and Juliet. Dir. Baz Luhrmann, 20th Century Fox, 1996.
V for Vendetta. Dir. James McTeigue, Warner Bros. Pictures, 2006.

Videos

BANGTANTV. (2019). *180511 RM*. [Video file]. Retrieved from <https://youtu.be/XZkfFD08zio>
BANGTANTV. (2019). *[2019 FESTA] BTS (*방탄소년단*)* '방탄다락' *#2019BTSFESTA*. [Video file]. Retrieved from <https://youtu.be/CPW2PCPYzEE>
BANGTANTV. (2018). BTS (방탄소년단) '방탄회식' #2018BTSFESTA. [Video file]. Retrieved from <https://youtu.be/K4Melso7MPU>
BANGTANTV. (2013). *130113 RAP MONSTER*. [Video file]. Retrieved from <https://youtu.be/3OMiM90b3IQ>
Big Hit Labels. (2020). *Big Hit corporate briefing with the community* (1H 2020). [Video file]. Retrieved from <https://youtu.be/WukUBUApb2U>
BTS. (2019). Ep. 1 Challenge. *Bring the soul: Docu-series*. [Vi-

deo file].

BTS. (2019). *It's been forever, too.* [Video file]. Retrieved from <https://www.vlive.tv/video/165723>

BTS. (2019). *BTS live: After a happy time, a relaxed glass.* [Video file]. Retrieved from <https://www.vlive.tv/video/134733>

Cestlavie9090. (2020). *Art world Berlin: Showcase.* [Video file]. Retrieved from <https://twitter.com/cestlavie9090/status/1218550668501274630>

Grammy Museum. (2018). *BTS-GRAMMY museum full conversation.* [Video file]. Retrieved from <https://www.facebook.com/grammymuseum/videos/498570413954851/>

Mnet K-POP. (2019). BTS(방탄소년단) at 2019 MAMA all moments. [Video file]. Retrieved from <https://youtu.be/Qrcr4gJWehU>

The Asian Theory. (2019). *9 K-Pop demographics that will change the way you see K-Pop.* [Video file]. Retrieved from <https://youtu.be/YDFvh_Dy0Kw>

UNICEF. (2018). *BTS speech at the United Nations/UNICEF.* [Video file]. Retrieved from <https://youtu.be/oTe4f-bBE-Kg>

Music Videos

Big Hit Labels. (2019). *BTS (*방탄소년단*) MAP OF THE SOUL: PERSONA. Persona comeback trailer.* [Video file]. Retrieved from <https://youtu.be/M9Uy0opVF3s>

Big Hit Labels. (2018). *BTS (*방탄소년단*) IDOL. Official MV.* [Video file]. Retrieved from <https://youtu.be/pBuZE-GYXA6E>

Big Hit Labels. (2017). *BTS (*방탄소년단*) DNA. Official MV.* [Video file]. Retrieved from <https://youtu.be/MBdVXkSdhwU>

Big Hit Labels. (2016). *BTS (*방탄소년단*) 피 땀 눈물 Blood*

Sweat & Tears. Official MV. [Video file]. Retrieved from <https://youtu.be/hmE9f-TEutc>

Big Hit Labels. (2015). *BTS (*방탄소년단*) I NEED U. Official MV (Original ver.).* [Video file]. Retrieved from <https://youtu.be/jjskoRh8GTE>

BTS WORLD Official. (2019). *BTS* (방탄소년단) *Heartbeat (BTS WORLD LOST MV.* [Video file]. Retrieved from <https://youtu.be/aKSxbt-O6TA>

Influential works

I was careful not to include in-text references as to not detract from the aesthetic and flow of logic for the reader. As such, I refrained from calling on too many academic works as this book is to serve as an introductory text. Those who I directly referenced have been highly influential, in particular: Dorothy Tennov, Simone de Beauvoir, Martin Buber, and, of course, BTS. These theorists, and BTS as artists, provide the backbone for my own theory and creative development. This allows me to reach through time and space in order to conceptualise a new way of being for idol and fan. Though not directly referenced in this book, I would like to acknowledge the often profound influence the following works and people have had in the development of my theories and creative expression.

The elementary forms of religious life by Émile Durkheim
Thanks to yet another old white dead guy for giving me the thought that started it all as I sat in my first sociology course in 2012. It was while studying Durkheim that I saw the link between religion and celebrity as a reflection of community, society and self which is celebrated and worshipped. How people often come together to pray to find themselves, much like how fans congregate at concerts and revel in the light of love shining from their idol. This began my eight year journey to conceptua-

lising experiences I hoped to be universal, both highly personal and incredibly political in nature.

The revolutionary social worker: The love ethic model by Dyann Ross
From your PhD in 2002, to your first solo book in 2020; you have shown me what love as an action is. After reading this book you commented that my concept of love 'is a bit out there'. I would like to take this opportunity to point out that yours is, too. We both write about the transformative power of love in action, love shared amongst humanity and extending to all living beings as equals. Of course, this is no mistake; this has been your life's work, and my lifetime of learning from you. Though I'm sure many people were concerned I had deviated from the path you laid before me, the apple hasn't fallen very far from the tree, after all. I just had to do it on my own terms. A highschool dropout who doesn't reference in-text and uses Harry Potter to explain theorised functions of the collective unconscious. Thank you for giving me the time and space to be me, even when I had no idea who that was. I know now.

Mono, a playlist by RM
I must admit, when I first heard Mono I thought it was awfully melancholy and saved it for long walks on rainy days. In hindsight, I was not ready. However, after my return from Writers' Residency in September 2019, I was thrown into a new kind of inner turmoil as I embarked on writing this book. Only then was I finally able to receive the comfort I believe you set out to deliver with this playlist. I hope the next time you release something of your own you call it for what it is; an EP, an album. I look forward to seeing you continue to step into and claim your power as an artist, a revolutionary, a human *dasein*. Thank you, for everything.

Made in the USA
Middletown, DE
20 August 2021